Patrick Francis Mullany

The development of English literature

The old english period

Patrick Francis Mullany

The development of English literature
The old english period

ISBN/EAN: 9783741190674

Manufactured in Europe, USA, Canada, Australia, Japa

Cover: Foto ©Andreas Hilbeck / pixelio.de

Manufactured and distributed by brebook publishing software (www.brebook.com)

Patrick Francis Mullany

The development of English literature

THE DEVELOPMENT

OF

ENGLISH LITERATURE:

The Old English Period.

BY

BROTHER AZARIAS,

OF THE BROTHERS OF THE CHRISTIAN SCHOOLS; PROFESSOR OF ENGLISH
LITERATURE IN ROCK HILL COLLEGE, MARYLAND; AUTHOR
OF A PHILOSOPHY OF LITERATURE.

Semper aut discere, aut docere, aut scribere dulce habui   BEDA.

NEW YORK:
D. APPLETON AND COMPANY,
549 AND 551 BROADWAY.
1879.

COPYRIGHT BY
D. APPLETON AND COMPANY,
1879.

PREFACE.

THE present volume traces the growth and development of Old English Thought as expressed in Old English Literature, from the first dawnings of history down to the Norman Conquest. It goes back of the written word to the life, the aspirations, and the motives that gave it expression. It seeks in the manners and customs, the religion and law and government and international relations of the Old English people, the sources whence the literature of that people derives its tone and coloring. For this purpose, the author has laid every available source of information under contribution. Dry land-grants, antiquated law-codes, the decrees of councils, the lives of saints, legend and history, the researches of scholar and critic and antiquarian, have all of them directly or indirectly been brought to bear upon the subject, and have been made use of to throw light upon the purely literary document.

PREFACE.

Intending the work for a class-book, the author has restricted himself to presenting the merest outline of his subject. He leaves it to the teacher to fill in whatever details are lacking. This volume is to be followed, as soon as precarious health permits, by two others in which it is proposed to bring the subject down to the present day.

Rock Hill College, *June* 2, 1879.

CONTENTS.

	PAGE
INTRODUCTION	1

CHAPTER I.

THE CONTINENTAL HOMESTEAD	5
I. English and Aryan	5
II. Soil, Climate, and Character	8
III. Laws and Customs	12
IV. Condition of Woman	23
V. The Mead-Hall	30
VI. Language and Poetry	33
VII. Philosophy	47

CHAPTER II.

KELTIC INFLUENCE	57
I. Kelt and Teuton	57
II. Kymric Kelt	61
III. Gaedhil and Kymry	68
IV. Keltic Sentiment	72

CHAPTER III.

THE OLD CREED AND THE NEW	77
I. The English in their Insular Homestead	77
II. Gregory the Great	79
III. Augustin and Paulinus	84
IV. Relapse and Recovery	88
V. Shadow and Substance	91

CONTENTS.

CHAPTER IV.

	PAGE
WHITBY	97
I. St. Hilda	97
II. The Story of Cedmon's Life Unraveled	100
III. The Themes Cedmon Sang	106
IV. The Secret of Cedmon's Success	110
V. Cedmon at Work	114
VI. Cedmon's Influence at Home and Abroad	123

CHAPTER V.

CANTERBURY	131
I. Theodore and Aldhelm	131
II. The Poem of Andreas	136
III. Cynewulf	141
IV. The Poems of Judith, Guthlac, and a Lover's Message	148

CHAPTER VI.

JARROW AND YORK	153
I. Benedict Biscop	153
II. Beda	154
III. Alcwin	161
IV. Popular Philosophy	164
V. The Reflective Mood in Poetry	171

CHAPTER VII.

WINCHESTER	175
I. Alfred the Great	175
II. Spirit of Laws	180
III. The Sentiment of Nationality	186

CHAPTER VIII.

ABINGDON	193
I. The Two Alfrics	194
II. Tenth Century Poetry	200
CONCLUSION	206

THE DEVELOPMENT
OF
ENGLISH LITERATURE.

INTRODUCTION.

1. A PEOPLE's literature is a criterion of a people's civilization. It embodies what is most enduring in thought, and records what is best worth remembering in deeds. A people may be conquered; it may lose its individuality; it may change its religion, its government, its soil; but so long as its literature remains, its growth and development, its rise and fall, its character and genius continue objects of interest and teach a lesson to all who wish to be instructed.

2. But literature is not all a people's thought. It is only that which a people regards as its best and most cherished thought. Thought has various forms of expression. It is embodied in a people's laws and manner of life, in its arts and architecture, in its philosophy and religion, in its politics, its science, and its industry. The idioms of its language speak of the richness or the poverty of its thought. Literature, then, is one among many forms of thought. That which one man writes out, another lives out. The idea expressed in a poem may be constructed in marble, or put upon canvas. Each form of expression throws light on the other.

3. Literature is the outcome of the whole life of a people. It is the creature of its day. To understand it aright, it must be studied in connection with the sources and influences that shape it. To consider it apart from these were to misapprehend its nature and its bearing. It were to lose sight of the real character of thought. Thought is as subtle as the spirit that gives it existence. It pervades every action of life. It is the indispensable accompaniment of all that man wills and does. It suggests his plans; it gives direction to his deeds; it regulates his industries; it molds his religion; it underlies his mythologies and superstitions; it explains his views; it sings of his heroic feats; it gives wings to his noblest aspirations. Man is so called because of his thinking power.[1]

4. Thought is modified by circumstances. It gets its shape from the place and time in which it is expressed; it receives its coloring from the person by whom it is spoken. No thought stands alone. It forms an inseparable link between those that have gone before and those that come after. A sentence expressing a living thought, spoken or written at a given time and in a given place, would at no other time and in no other place receive the exact form it receives then and there. Nor could other than the person speaking or writing it give it the same tone as that it takes.

5. As with a single sentence, so is it with a whole literature. Time, and place, and person, and manner, and matter should all be duly considered. According to the degree of a people's civilization, its political and social position, its natural aptitude, and its educational facilities, will it express itself. The stage of its growth is to be taken into account. At no two epochs of its

---

[1] The word *man* is pure Sanskrit, and means *to think*.

social and political life will it use the same form of utterance.

6. The history of a people's literature, then, is inseparable from that of a people's life. It traces the growth and development of the one and the other from the first dawnings of time, and calls attention to influences on other peoples, and other peoples' influences upon them. It is the aim of the present work so to tell the history of English literature. It begins by describing English character, and English thought, as they exist when first the English people comes upon the arena of history. It then considers the growth and development of that thought, and that character, as they expand under the influences of Kelt, Roman, Dane, and Norman, and are fostered by the teachings of Christianity. It seeks the life-thoughts of an author in his works, and of an epoch in its literature.

7. Throughout the present work this canon of criticism is the guiding principle: part of a people's literature is common to the human race; another part is common to the family of races to which the people belongs; still another part is peculiar to one or other of these races, and borrowed from them; the residue is the people's own. And of this residue a portion is impersonal, and belongs to the age in which it is expressed; the remainder is personal, and peculiar to the individual.

CHAPTER I.

THE CONTINENTAL HOMESTEAD.

THREE neighboring races invaded the island of Britain. They found it occupied by a kindred race known as the Kelt. After a long and fierce struggle they established themselves upon the island, drove the greater part of the natives to the west, where they became known to them as Welsh or aliens,[1] subjugated others, and finally imposed upon all their laws and government. In their Continental homestead they were known as Jutes, Saxons, and Angles or English ; in their new insular home they called themselves Englishmen and their language English.[2] As such they will be known to us from the beginning. All three races are of the same stock, having the same religion, ruled by the same laws and customs, and speaking the same language. Let us determine their intellectual and social standing prior to their making the conquest of England.

I.—ENGLISH AND ARYAN.

The English inhabited that part of Europe now known as the Schleswig-Holstein provinces and the

---

[1] Wealas—Wälsch—Walloon—strangers.
[2] *Englisc.* The term *Anglo-Saxon* is of modern date.

Netherlands. This was their second homestead. Many centuries previously they lived in their cradle-land in Asia. They bear kinship with the Persian and Hindu ; but their difference of occupation, the nature of their soil, and the influence of climate so changed their natures, and gave such direction to their thoughts, that it were difficult to imagine them originally one people with the Hindu, did they not retain evidence of the relationship in their language. And that proves them to be of the same stock. In both do we find words identical in sound and in meaning, as the term *naman*, which means " name " both in Sanskrit and old English.[1] Sometimes, while the word remains, its primitive meaning becomes changed in one or other of the languages. Such is the word *path*, which as a verb means " to go."[2] In this sense is it used by Shakespeare, in a passage over which the critics have been greatly exercised :

"For, if thou path, thy native semblance on,
Not Erebus itself were dim enough
To hide thee from prevention."[3]

It is the privilege of genius to strike the original meaning of a word long after it has passed from the common intelligence. Such was Shakespeare's in this instance. Again, in our irregular verbs, we have forms which can be accounted for only by a comparative study of the Sanskrit. Take, for instance, the verb *to be*. The forms *is* and *am* come from the verb *as*, of the same meaning, and its first person singular, *asmi* ; the form *was* is found in the verb *vas*, to dwell ; and the

See Bosworth's *Anglo-Saxon and English Dictionary*, p. 171, and Max Müller's *Sanskrit Grammar*, p. 87.
[2] Benfey's *Sanskrit English Dictionary*, p. 508.
[3] *Julius Cæsar*, Act ii., sc. 1.

form *be* is one with *bhu*, a word having also the same meaning.[1] And it is only in a language cognate to the Sanskrit that we find the root-word of our comparative *better*. "In the Persian," says Cardinal Wiseman, "we have precisely the same comparative, *behter*, with exactly the same signification, regularly formed from its positive *beh*, good; just as we have in the same language *badter*, worse, from *bad*."[2]

The English, then, are a branch of the Aryan family. That primitive people, the mother race of Kelt and Teuton and Hindu, was devoted to the cultivation of the soil; the English have, at all times, shown a fondness for the tillage of the land, except when brought face to face with almost insurmountable difficulties, as the encroachments of the sea. That mother race was passionately attached to Nature-worship; the English retained that inherited love for Nature. They deified the elements, even as did their sister peoples, the Greeks and Hindus, and as did their Aryan mother prior to either. With impetuous feelings rushed they to the hunt; with reckless eagerness they committed themselves to the mercy of wind and wave. The Aryan was a people fond of philosophical speculation; the common problems and the nearly common solutions, inherited by the Aryan nations, prove as much. But the English of old became too besotted with heavy and coarse drinks, which they indulged in to excess, to be able to speculate with the acuteness of Greek or Hindu. With the Aryan, home was a sacred refuge, and all the family relations were held in reverence as well as honor; this became, with the English, one of their most widely

[1] See Max Müller's *Sanskrit Grammar* for each of these verbs, pp. 277, 260, 245.
[2] *Lectures on Science and Revealed Religion*, Lect. i., p. 30.

cherished and deeply rooted sentiments. The Ayran fell under the influences of his senses, to the clouding of his spiritual parts ; so were the English greatly wrapped up in their material natures. The Aryan was given to poetry in which man and nature were blended ; so were the English, but with a difference. Living in the land of the sunny East, the ancestral race rejoiced in the harmonies and beauties of form and color ; but in their woody, mist-enveloped land, the English lost sight of these things, and they ceased to be for them what they were for the Kelt and the Greek, a passion.

II.—Soil, Climate, and Character.

In their Continental homestead, the English lived and worked and had their aspirations and their opinions of things. To understand aright the Englishman of modern history, we must observe him as he was two thousand years ago. We must learn his ways and penetrate his thoughts. National traits of character are not the work of a day ; they are the outcome of centuries of slow, persistent action. Man begins by accommodating himself to circumstances ; this is the first step he takes in the formation of his manhood. Circumstances in their turn react upon him, his thoughts, his ways, his dispositions ; this gives the final direction to character, suggests divergence from the early home-life, and creates a new type of race. In general, the nature of the soil will determine the occupations of a people ; its occupations will give color and shape to its thoughts ; they, in turn, will mold the expression of its literature. The native land of the Old English was a land of fog and mist, of fat, muddy soil, and of slow, sluggish rivers. It was covered with vast forests. It was a land on which the sea was ever making encroachments; and in this respect it is still the same land. Witness the untiring exertions of Holland to repel these encroachments, and to recover lost ground, by her system of dikes. But in the days of which we speak there were no dikes. The result was, that at the equinoxes the whole country became suddenly submerged, and as suddenly the water subsided. Tacitus describes the country under one of these visitations: "The wind blowing hard from the north, and the waves, as usual at the equinox, rolling with a prodigious swell, . . . the country was laid under water. The sea, the shore, and the fields presented one vast expanse. The depths and shallows, the quicksands and the solid ground, were no more distinguished. . . . The return of day presented a new phase of things : the waters had subsided and the land appeared."[1] A people so situated must needs accommodate itself to the sea, and make it yield profit in proportion to the destruction it deals. On this principle acted the Old English. They not only became accustomed to the sea; they loved it; their greatest pleasure they found in sporting in its waves. Their little boats of hide danced about upon its rugged bosom as though they were things of life. Beowulf would have been considered no fit hero for an Old English poem, had he not, when a youth, ventured on the stormy ocean; and so we find him in friendly competition with Brecca, striving to perform feats of valor. Hunferth speaks :

"Then on the sound ye rowed, and thence with arms
The ocean covered, and the sea-streets measured;
With hands ye gripped and glided o'er the main;

[1] *Annals*, B. i., chap. 70.

With winter's fury boiled the waves o' the deep;
While on the waters toiled ye seven nights."[1]

But the sea was not only a pleasure for this people; it was the sole inheritance of the younger members of a family. They had no share in the land. They had to win for themselves a livelihood and a position in society. They were regarded as *wargrs*, wolves, outlaws. It is related that every five years the Scandinavians sent away their adult sons, reserving only those who were to perpetuate the family. "The wargr shakes dust on his father and mother, throws an herb over his shoulders, and with a bound clearing the inclosure of his paternal property, he seeks adventures afar."[2] There are generally others of the same age and condition to accompany him. And with light heart and cheery voice they cast their boats upon the water and make their home thereon for years to come. They live by plunder and piracy. "They overcome all who have the courage to oppose them. They surprise all who are so imprudent as not to be prepared for their attack. When they pursue they infallibly overtake; when they are pursued their escape is certain. They despise danger; they are inured to shipwreck; they are eager to purchase booty with the peril of their lives. Tempests, which to others are so dreadful, to them are subjects of joy." Such is the picture drawn of them by Sidonius;[3] nor is it overcol-

---

[1] thá git on sund reón, thær git eagor-stream,
earmum théhton, mæton mere-stráeta,
mundum brugdon, glidon ofer gársecg;
geofon ythum weol, wintres wylme;
git on waeteres æht seofon-niht swuncon.—
Beowulf, viii., 1029–1038.

[2] Cæsar Cantù, *Histoire Universelle*, vol. vii.

[3] viii., 6; Lingard, vol. i., p. 75.

ored. They were the terror of the sea. They were as cruel and fierce as they were adventurous. They only respected the fierceness and lawlessness as great as their own. They put the vanquished to death. While their neighbors, the Visigoths, were content with two thirds of the property,¹ nothing short of extermination seemed to satisfy them. It is to be expected that such a stormy life would render any other mode of living tame and monotonous. (So we find them when in trouble seeking solace in the pleasures of the ocean.) (Thus, Ragnar Lodbrok loses his wife in death. He leaves his government and his children in care of guardians, and betakes himself to a life of piracy, "that in the society of his vikings he might drown or mitigate his sorrow for one whom he has so tenderly loved."²) Here are the forefathers of the Drakes and the Raleighs. (This manner of living establishes bravery alone as the ideal of life.)* Wisdom and prudence were only secondary by side of this one quality. Sörli and Hamdir go to avenge the fate of their sister. On their way they meet their brother Erp. They ask him what help he would give them in their enterprise. He tells them that as hand helps hand and foot helps foot, so will he help them. His prudent and truly wise answer is not in accordance with their fierce mood; they slay him and repent their rashness at leisure.³ Could a people warring in such a spirit know mercy? No wonder that Urien calls Idda and his twelve sons firebrands.⁴

[1] Cæsar Cantù, vol. vii., p. 286.
[2] Thorpe, *Northern Mythology*, vol. i., p. 109.
[3] Thorpe, *loc. cit.*, p. 108.
[4] Flamddwyn.

III.—Laws and Customs.

While the vikings developed the spirit of war, plunder, piracy, and rash bravery, their brothers at home had their own peculiar way of living. But it was not altogether a lawless one. It was not as the dumb and low herd. Wherever we fall upon a number of men we find them an organized society, living together in obedience to known and recognized laws and customs, and each prepared to sacrifice to a certain extent his own ease and happiness for the public good. Such was the condition of the Old English. Their first social bond was one of blood. They ranged themselves according to kinship. They were divided into companies of ten men, each of whom pledged himself to obtain reparation from him who violated the common peace. This was called a *tithing*. Each tithing had for head a *tungéréfa*. Every ten tithings was called a *hundred* among the Saxons, and *wapen-tæce* among the English. The hundreds were under a *géréfa*. Several hundreds composed a shire, *scir*, commanded by a *scirgéréfa*.[1] Every man was thus bound up with every other man in mutual protection. He inherited the land to improve and defend it. To abandon it was considered a crime. The Salic Law[2] forbids a citizen to leave his birthplace without the consent of every other citizen in it. The Lombard Law of Luitprand pronounces penalty of death on the one attempting to leave the kingdom.[3] And such, no doubt, was the universal custom in the mother-homes of these barbarians. They had an hereditary nobility; but their king seems to have been chosen from among the ablest of their chiefs, according to cir-

---
[1] Whence our word *sheriff*. [2] Titre, xlvii.
[3] Lib. iii., art. iv.

cumstances. Beda says of the ancient English that "they have no king, but several lords who rule their nation; and when a war happens they cast lots indifferently, and on whomsoever the lot falls him they follow and obey during the war; but, as soon as the war is ended, all these lords are again equal in power."[1] This assertion might hold true of the marauding expeditions; it might even exactly represent the condition of the Teuton races at certain epochs; but it was not anciently universal. When Beda wrote these nations were in the condition of the Greeks under an oligarchy, as Corinth under the Bacchiadæ, and Athens under the Eupatridæ. But Tacitus tells us that in his day the kings were chosen from the nobility;[2] and this assertion of Mr. Henry Sumner Maine is confirmed by history: "With the differences, however, that in the East aristocracies became religious, in the West civil or political, the proposition that an historical era of aristocracies succeeded an historical era of heroic kings may be considered as true, if not of all mankind, at all events of all branches of the Indo-European family of nations."[3] But the kings were among the Old English limited in their jurisdiction by the nobility. These met in council, in the *gauding*,[4] and framed the laws that were considered needful for the people.[5] At a later date this same assembly will be known as the Upper House of Parlia-

[1] B. v., ch. 10.
[2] "Reges ex nobilitate, duces ex virtute sumunt."—*Germania*, ch.vii.
[3] *Ancient Law*, p. 11.
[4] From *gau*, a canton, and *dingen*, to deliberate; hence the Old English word *thing*, meaning an assembly or judgment-room. Our modern husting is *hûs-thing*.
[5] Dans le prologue des lois des angles, il est dit qu'elles sont faites *omnium consensu*. Cantù, *Hist. Un.*, t. viii., p. 308. See the introduction to Alfred's laws.

ment. And among the nobility one there was who was the chosen confidant, the knower of secrets, *rún-wita*, and the counselor, *ráed-bora*, as was Æschere that of Hrothgar.[1] He will afterward be known in mediæval times as the king's favorite, and in modern times as the prime minister.

The Old English recognized two orders of society, the bond and the free. Possession of a certain amount of land was the indispensable condition of a freeman. "All that we learn," says Kemble, "of the original principles of settlement, prevalent either in England or on the Continent of Europe, among the nations of Germanic blood, rests upon two foundations: first, the possession of land; second, the distinction of rank; and the public law of every Teutonic tribe implies the dependence of one upon the other principle to a greater or less extent."[2] This was the animating principle of conquest among the English both in their old and new homes. He was nothing who possessed not land. Life was not worth the having without it; therefore, the landless one was prepared to stake his all in its acquisition. He lives to acquire wealth and power; he acquires wealth and power to be held in estimation. For this purpose each chief has with him a certain number of companions who are pledged to stand by him under all circumstances; to fight with him shoulder to shoulder in combat; to avenge his death, and on no account to survive his fall in the fray. This was so in the days of Tacitus. He tells us that he who survived his leader survived to live in infamy.[3] Death was considered preferable to

---

[1] *Beowulf*, ll., 269-70.

[2] *Saxons in England*, vol. i., chap. ii., p. 35.

[3] "Jam vero infame in omnem vitam ac probrosum, superstitem principi suo ex acie recessisse."—*Mor. Germ.*, xiv.

LAWS AND CUSTOMS.

such a life. Wiglaf reproaches the followers of Beowulf for surviving their prince and for their cowardice in not helping him to fight the firedrake; and he adds the penalty:

> "By our land's rights must each man of the tribe
> . Idly wander forth; then nobles from afar
> Your banishment, inglorious deed, shall learn.
> *Far better death than live a life of blame.*"[1]

This sentiment they brought with them to their British home. At the death of Byrhtnoth, which occurred about the year 991 A. D., many of the leaders express their resolution to die with their slain chief, while they execrate one they had seen fly. One "vowed in haughty words that he would not yield a foot's breadth of earth, nor turn his back in flight since his superior lay dead."[2]

The freemen were divided into eorls and ceorls. In their language manhood was identified with eorlship.[3] Of the eorls there were two classes: the ethelings or nobles, who enjoyed liberty, the right of holding property, and the power of jurisdiction; and the ahrimans, who were excluded from the *malls* or deliberative assemblies and cultivated the soil. They need not go to war; they were free to pay a sum of money and supply provisions in the stead. The ceorls or tributaries possess individual liberty, but they are alienated with

[1] lond-rihtes mót
thære mæg-burge monna æghwylc
idel hweorfan, syththan æthelingas
feórran gefricgean fleám eowerne,
dómleásan dæd. *Dedth bith sélla
eorla gehwylcum thonne edwit-lif.—Beowulf,* xxxix., 5765, *et seq.*
[2] Death of Byrhtnoth. Conybeare's *Anglo-Saxon Poetry.*
[3] *Eorlscipe* is manliness, courage. See Bosworth's *Anglo-Saxon and English Dictionary.*

the lands on which they live.¹ Impoverished proprietors who found themselves unable to respond to the heriban, or call to arms, frequently renounced their civil rights and placed themselves under the protection of a richer proprietor.² The serfs or slaves had no rights or privileges. Their master held over them the power of life and death. He was responsible for them as he was for the cattle of his field. If their master was held amenable before the law, they were to pay the fines for him. In time of war, if it was considered expedient to make them fight, they were liberated, as it was only a freeman who could bear arms.

Nearly all crimes could be compensated for by the payment of a certain sum of money. The only exceptions were treason, desertion, and poison. These involved capital punishment, and the sentence was pronounced, not by the chief, but by the priest. He was the more immediate representative of the Author of life and death. This sentiment might not be expressed; it certainly was implied. In case of homicide, which on account of excessive drinking and the custom of always bearing arms in public, was frequent, the family of the slain man might either accept the compensation-money, *mæg-bót*, or take upon themselves the avenging of his death. The individual did not stand alone upon his own responsibility. His kin were held accountable for his acts.³ And for every offense against person or property there was set down a fine. That against the person was called *werigeld;* that against property *widri-*

---

¹ Cantù, *Hist. Un.*, vii., p. 297.

² This was known as *mundebund*.

³ Thus, Ethelbihrt's laws decree that if a murderer leaves the country his kinsfolk shall pay half the fine. They are as early as 600. See Tacitus, *De Mor. Ger.*, xii.

geld.[1] These old law-makers went into all imaginable details. According to the tooth that was broken was a man fined. For the wounding of the finger, the hand, the arm, the head, the eye, the ear, was there a graded list of fines. So too for property. Every implement of agriculture, every domestic animal, every piece of furniture, had its set price, if stolen, injured, or broken. These laws they will afterward take with them into England, and they will be attributed to Ethelbirht, or Ini, or Hlothere, or more especially to Alfred. The unwritten custom may have existed for centuries prior to the written code. Laws are not invented, they grow out of circumstances. And in fact what is English law to-day but what it was under Alfred, what it had been in the Continental homestead, a tissue of particular rules based upon precedents; these precedents finally resolving themselves into a judgment passed on a particular case? There is no science, no digest of principles. The only improvement made upon the old order of things is that the laws have ceased to be a simple relation of man to man; and instead of being administered in the name of private revenge or personal satisfaction, they are laid down for justice's sake. The history of all law resolves itself into the recording of the process of this transformation. Formerly, society did not trouble itself about the individual, once he had paid the required amount to the king and the injured party.[2] Nowadays, it looks to his future good behavior. There is also a difference in the manner of proceeding. Then, the accused was presumed guilty till he proved himself otherwise; at present, the law regards him as innocent till he is proved guilty. To establish his innocence his own

---

[1] Grimm, *Deutschen Rechts-alterthümer*, 650.
[2] Tacitus, *Mor. Germ.*, xii., *Æthelbirhtes Dómás*, § 9, Ed. Schmid.

assertion was not enough. He got his neighbors and kinsmen to swear to the truth of a fact. In their British home, these neighbors will be set down as a fixed number; they will become the judges of the law in all important cases; and men will say that Alfred the Great organized them into a jury. We have here the germ of trial by jury, with all its advantages and disadvantages.

But in the old homestead there are other means for establishing the truth or falsity of an accusation. One of the most popular and universal among the Germanic nations was the duel. In English law it is known as the wager of battle. Velleius Paterculus speaks of disputes among the Germans which were wont to be determined by arms.[1] And he further says that they despised the Roman method of settling difficulties by the decisions of a law tribunal. Nor were the early Greeks and Romans without this means of determining guilt or innocence. Long after the practice had been abolished the word in which it was expressed remained. With both peoples the same word meant both to fight and to judge or determine.[2] This is to be looked for among a warlike people. And when to this is added a spirit of ferocious independence, such as burned in the breast of the whole Teutonic people, we have all the conditions favorable to making the duel a most popular mode of trial. The primary idea underlying this practice was expressed by Gondebaud in his reply to Avitus: "Is it not true that in the wars of nations, as in private combats, the issue is in the hand of God? And why will not His providence give victory to the justest cause?"[3] It is also true that to rely on God's direct interference

---

[1] Lib. ii., chap. 118; Blackstone, B. iii., § 337.
[2] Greek, κρίνειν; Latin, decernere.
[3] Cantù Hist. Un., t. vii., p. 333.

on all occasions is to tempt Him. However, the duel pleased their savage natures; they loved to witness it; they honored the champion; the coward who craved[1] for mercy they despised. This practice of the wager of battle will be introduced in the new home; it will be revived by William the Conqueror;[2] it will be appealed to in 1612 and 1631, and will be abolished only in 1817.[3]

Another form of proving one's guilt or innocence was the ordeal of fire and water. This was universal among the Aryan nations. We find it in India. The beautiful Sita proves her innocence by fire.[4] We find it in Greece. The messenger tells Creon that he and the watchman were ready to lift masses of red-hot iron in their hands, and to pass through the fire, and to appeal to the gods by oath that they had not buried Polynices.[5] To the Old English, to whom fire and water were not only elements but deities, this mode of appeal had its attractions. Surely the gods would not harm the innocent one who would commit himself to their mercies, as surely would they not let pass unpunished the guilty one placing himself in their power; therefore they placed confidence in this manner of trial.

Another feature of the Old English, and one which they shared in common with other Teutonic tribes, was their custom of possessing their lands in common, and moving about from place to place. "In cultivating the soil," says Tacitus, "they do not settle on one spot, but shift about different places." And Cæsar describes the

[1] Hence the word *craven;* Anglo-Saxon, *crafian.*
[2] Not *introduced,* as Blackstone has it. *Commentaries,* B. iii., § 338.
[3] 59 Geo. III., c. 46.
[4] Ramayana.
[5] Sophocles, *Antigone,* 262–266.

process : "The magistrates and chiefs parcel out yearly to the tribes and families united together such a quantity of land and in such part of the country as they deem proper, and the year after compel them to move elsewhere."[1] Thus they were taught not to become attached to any particular piece of land, lest their ambition and martial qualities lie dormant or fall into contempt. This reveals another trait in their manner of thinking. It was not this or that piece of land that was the object of their desires : it was land, property, not for its own sake, but as representative of their relative standing in their respective tribes. "The system of an annual changing," says Lappenberg, "or at least changeable possessions of land, and the custom necessarily attending it, of migrating, prejudicial as they were to the solid interests of nations, nevertheless required activity and strength of mind ; the individual, too, whose home afforded him no permanent settlement would not respect that of a stranger ; while piracy, ennobled by stratagem and valor, is indebted only to an established system of social order for its disgrace and punishment."[2] It was a system calculated to

---

[1] "Neque quisquam agri modum certum aut fines habet proprios, sed magistratus ac principes in annos singulos gentibus cognationibusque hominum, qui una colerunt, quantum et quo loco visum est agri attribuunt atque anno post alio transire cogunt."—*De Bello Gallico*, lib. vi., cap. 22. See also lib. iv., 1. The custom still exists in the Hochwald of Thor, except that the division is not made annually.— Lappenberg, ii., 323.

[2] *England under Anglo-Saxon Kings*, vol. i., p. 86. Professor Stubbs, with his usual felicity, thus expresses the relations of the proprietor to the land : "As the king is the king of the nation, not of the land, the land is rather the sign or voucher for the freedom of its possessor than the basis of his rights. He possesses his land as being a full, free member of the community ; henceforth the possession of it is the attes-

strengthen individual liberty. And everything in their customs and laws spoke of this sentiment. Each house stood apart, surrounded by a piece of land that was reserved for the use of the proprietor. No one dare enter without blowing a horn or giving some signal of his coming, otherwise he was regarded as an enemy, and was dealt by accordingly. Each village was constructed in the same manner. It was surrounded by a march or mark of land, which was regarded as sacred ground. He who would cross it, without giving a signal, was looked upon with suspicion, and his every movement watched. Everybody entering a house was received with hospitality. Food and drink were provided for him, and no questions asked till he was refreshed and rested. "To injure guests they regard as impious; they defend from harm those who have come to them for any purpose whatever, and esteem them inviolable; to them the houses of all are open, and maintenance freely supplied."[1] But the host was held responsible for the guest under his roof. On his departure, he accompanied him to the limits of his *vil*, not through motives of personal kindness or politeness, but to be sure that his guest committed no act for which he, as host, would have to suffer. In rehabilitating the Old English, we must in a great measure forget the amenities of modern life, and think of a people with a selfish nature uncontrolled by conventionalities. They were ferocious, and their ferociousness spoiled the good effects of the priceless liberty of which they were justly so jealous. It was a liberty totally regardless of time and place. We find the Saxon portion of the Teutonic race afterward carrying this spirit of personal liberty

tation, type, and embodiment of his freedom and political rights."— *Constitutional History of England*, vol. i., p. 50.

[1] Cæsar, *De Bel. Gal.*, lib. vi., cap. 23.

with them among other nations, to the extent that the Lombards had to enact a law banishing those Saxons who refused to abide by other than their own Saxon laws.[1]

The men went armed, and so universal was the custom, man came to be known as the weaponed one—*wæpned*. Thus, where the modern English use the terms male and female, their ancestors of old spoke of the *wæpned* and *wifman*.[2] In every public place went they in arms. Whenever they held a council, they did so armed. They looked more to the decoration of their shields than to the adorning of their persons. To lose them was a disgrace. They took the greatest pride in decorating them in variegated colors. In Beowulf, the shield is called a yellow disk—*geolo-rand*. They prized their shield and their sword or spear as the instruments of the sole occupation for which they lived. To war was their ideal of life. Even after death they could think of no higher form of existence than to drink beer in the halls of the Valhalla, and fight their battles daily over again. Therefore they never put forth their strength except in the battle-field. And then the energy they displayed was great. Nothing could resist it when under disciplined leadership. They became furious. They bit their shields and uttered the most horrid shrieks. They considered themselves under the immediate protection of the god of battle.[3] In their fury they played with life and death. War they regarded as a play. Their war-shield they called a play-shield—*plega-scyld*. And among their synonyms for war we find *æsc-plega*, the sport of lances or spears, and *hand-plega*, a

[1] Cæsar, Cantù, t. vii., p. 315.
[2] Akerman, *Remains of Pagan Saxondom.*
[3] Woden. Hence the old English word for madness, *wodnes*.

contest.[1] But, the war over, they became inactive. Occasionally they would hunt. They had a hound—a *ren-hund*—of which they were very fond. But, when not so engaged, they did nothing requiring physical exertion. "The intrepid warrior," says Tacitus, "who in the field braved every danger, became in time of peace a listless sluggard."[2] They were addicted to gambling. When they possessed naught else, they staked their persons and went into bondage to satisfy their creditors. They also gave days and nights to deep drinking. As a necessary consequence, quarrels were frequent and dangerous. "Disputes," to quote Tacitus again, "as will be the case with people in liquor, frequently arise, and are seldom confined to opprobrious language. The quarrel generally ends in a scene of blood."[3] In such a manner of living we look in vain for a guiding principle. There is no restraint on individual impulses. Spirit is entirely subject to physical instincts. But we get insight into the germs of those vices that have been the bane of so many individuals, and brought disaster upon so many families in the new homestead centuries after.

IV.—Condition of Woman.

Here it may be asked how a people so brutalized could hold woman in reverence, and regard marriage as a sacred institution. Still Tacitus tells us so.[4] But it is to be remembered that Tacitus is detailing the manners and customs of the Teutonic nations, not sim-

[1] See Bosworth's *Dictionary*.
[2] *De Mor. Germ.*, cap. xv.
[3] *Ibid*, xxii.
[4] "Quanquam severa illic matrimonia." *De Mor. Ger.*, xviii. "Paucissima in tam numerosa gente adulteria; quorum pœna præsens et maritis permissa." *Ibid.*, xix.

ply as a matter of history, but as a rebuke to Roman corruption. He therefore writes with more point than history warrants. In his desire to contrast he exaggerates. The Teuton of old led a life of hardship. His was a simple mode of living. He knew few of the luxuries of an Oriental or a Roman civilization. His sluggish nature retained all its innate vigor. There was in his daily life nothing to enervate him and render him effeminate. But he entertained for woman no chivalric sense of delicacy. A creature of impulses, he was incapable of restraint. He guarded her virtue simply through the motive of right and property which were vested in her. His sense of independence could not brook encroachments upon his possessions, whether of person or property. Hence he hedged woman in with laws that were as wounding to her modesty as they were derogatory to her honor. They ignored her personality. They guarded her as they would have guarded a pet animal or a fruit-bearing tree. Thus was it enacted that the freeman who presses the finger of a freewoman is liable to a fine of six hundred pence; of twelve hundred if he touches the arm; of fourteen hundred if he places his hand above the elbow; and so on through a grade of fines, entering into details as disgusting as they must have been futile. Nor were these laws confined to the Old English and their neighbors. They were generally used throughout the Teutonic races. In the Bavarian laws, he who disarranges a woman's hair or detaches her comb is fined a certain amount.[1] Legislation on such a subject, entering into such minute details, taking such stringent measures, implies great abuse, and proves conclusively that woman was not the object of respect to the ancient Teuton which some

[1] Cœsar Cantù, *Histoire Universelle*, t. vii., p. 379.

would make her, and that she was simply cared for because she was to be the mother of the young heroes and vikings who were to perpetuate the name and the prowess of their fathers. Commenting on the punishment inflicted on the woman unfaithful to her husband, as related by Tacitus, namely, that her hair was cut, and she was whipped ignominiously through the village,[1] Balmes remarks : " Certainly, this punishment gives us an idea of the infamy which was attached to adultery among the Germans, but it was little calculated to increase the respect entertained for woman publicly. This would have been greater had she been stoned to death."[2]

Be this as it may, the more we study the condition of woman in those early days, the less pleasing a picture does it present. She was the companion of man in war, and his slave in peace ; she attended to all the indoor and outdoor work ;[3] while he sat dozing in half-stupor by the fire she was up and doing ; she accompanied him to the battle-field ; she stood by his side and encouraged him in moments of greatest danger. Living in such slavishness, she lost all the finer instincts of her womanly nature. The ideal woman of the Sagas of the North is one bloodthirsty, cruel, cold, heartless, and fatally beautiful. In the Völsung Saga, Signi counsels Sigmund to destroy her own children, since he does not consider them valiant enough.[4] " The daughter of the Danish jarl, seeing Egil taking his seat near her, repels him with scorn, reproaching him with seldom having provided the wolves with hot meat, with never having seen for a whole autumn a raven croaking over the carnage. But Egil seized her, and pacified her, by sing

---

[1] *De Mor. Ger.*, cap. xix.   [2] *European Civilization*, chap. xxvii.
[3] *De Mor. Ger.*, cap. xv.   [4] Sæmunda's Edda.

ing : 'I have marched with my bloody sword, and the raven has followed me. Furiously we fought; the fire passed over the dwellings of men; we slept in the blood of those who kept the gate.'"[1] Such is this maiden's ideal of a hero and of life. A fancy so steeped in carnage and crime could be possessed of a small share of tenderness and humanity. Nor is the ideal woman of the Nibelungen-lied less fierce. Brunhild forces her suitors to contend with her in the games of throwing the spear, leaping, and hurling the stone, under the barbarous penalty of losing their heads in case of defeat. She afterward has Siegfried slain; in return, his wife, Crimhild, after brooding over her wrongs for years, revenges herself by slaying his murderer. She is possessed of as little humanity as her rival. She asks Hagen where the fatal Hoard is; Hagen replies that he never will disclose it while any of her brothers lives, whereupon she orders her brother's head to be cut off, and, holding it up, exclaims, "I bring it to an end." "Thou hast it now according to thy will," said Hagen; " of the Hoard knoweth none but God and I; from thee, she-devil— *Valendinne*— shall it for ever be hid." In her rage she kills him with her own hand.[2] Not in representations like these are we to find the ideal of true womanhood. Such characters bear no other traces of their sex than the name, and woman unsexed is a monster. No surprise is it, then, to read of the English lady of primitive times cruel to her servants and slaves.[3] The types set

---

[1] Apud Taine, vol. i., p. 27.

[2] *Nibelungen-lied*, ed. Simrock, p. 383. See also Carlyle's Essay on Van der Hagen's edition of this poem.

[3] Wright's *History of Domestic Manners and Sentiments in the Middle Ages*, p 58.

up for her admiration were such as belittled the tenderness and delicacy of feeling and thought that belong to true wifely, motherly, and sisterly qualities. The Edda has summed up the Teutonic estimate of woman in these words: "Praise a woman when she is buried . . . praise a maiden after she is married."[1] This is denying her all merit. But later woman will be emancipated; her rights and privileges will be recognized; she will be restored to full liberty of action; a halo of tenderness will be woven about her name; the day will come when she will no longer be ignored as heir to her father's property, and we will read among the formulas of Marculf a deed proclaiming that, as the Lord has given a father daughters as well as sons, who love him as well as they, he sets aside the former impious custom, and wills that after death they share equally in the goods he leaves.[2] But, before this change takes place, the whole framework of society must be altered. Under the old order of things woman does not inherit because she is unable to bear the responsibilities attached thereto, for with the property inherited came also the feuds, the avenging of injuries, and the vengeance to be taken for homicide,[3] but in the new order, men will have other things to live for than war and vengeance. The power that will bring about that change is Christianity.

[1] *Hava-Mal.*

[2] "Dulcissimæ filiæ N. N. diuturna sed impia inter nos consuetudo tenetur, ut de terra paterna sorores cum fratribus portionem non habeant. Sed ego, perpendens hanc impietatem, sicut mihi a Domino æqualiter donati estis filii, ita sitis a me æqualiter diligendi, et de rebus meis post decessum æqualiter gratulemini."

[3] Thus the Thuringian law is explicit on this point: "Ad quemcumque hæreditas terræ pervenerit ad illum vestis bellica, id est lorica, et ultio proximi, et solutio leudis debit pertinere."—Canciani. *Leg. Barb.*, tit. iii., art. 5, p. 31.

Among the well-to-do class of the Old English, from the second to the fifth centuries, woman's chief occupation was, what it afterward became in the new homestead, spinning, weaving, and embroidering. The fine for injury done the hands of a goldsmith and embroideress was great.[1] These two vocations were held in esteem. It is proof that gold and embroidered ornaments were manufactured and held in request. In Beowulf, the palace is variegated with gold—*gold-fáh;*[2] the boar's likeness that the men bear on their cheeks is *gehroden golde*[3]—adorned with gold; Hengist's band should supply as much treasure of rich gold—*fœttan goldes*—as would decorate the Frisian race in the beer-hall;[4] Wealthow walks forth under a golden diadem—*gyldnum beáge;*[5] Hæreth's daughter is given, gold-adorned—*gold-hroden*—to the young warrior;[6] whence we learn that men and women both used ornaments of gold. But this was after the days of Tacitus, for he tells us that the use of gold and silver was unknown to them, with the exception of those who had come in contact with Roman civilization. Every house was divided into two parts, the beer-hall or reception-room for strangers and guests, and the female apartments, exclusively used by the women. These were not always contiguous. "For others," says Wright, and his description holds true for the Continental home as well as for the British, "and for the ladies especially, little rooms were built outside, often standing apart from any other building; and the Anglo-Saxons called this room a *bur*, which in our change of language answers to our *bower*."[7] There

---

[1] Lappenberg, i., 94.
[2] *Beowulf*, l., 621.
[3] l., 614.
[4] l., 2190.
[5] l., 2330.
[6] l., 3900.
[7] *Homes of Other Days*, p. 4.

they sewed, and with their servants and slaves attended to their spinning and embroidery. But they ate with the men in the large hall. When Ragnar visited his friend Öston, at Upsala, the King's daughter went around the hall presenting mead and wine to Ragnar and his men.[1] Rowena gives the cup to Vortigern "with all the grace and neatness that might be, according to the fashion of her country."[2] At the feast given to Beowulf, where he never saw greater joy, the Queen, Wealthow, was present, and "at times surveyed the hall," while Hrothgar's daughter from time to time bore the ale-cup to the earls.[3] And on the day of his arrival Wealthow greeted the men in the hall, mindful of their kin—*cynna gemyndig*—and first gave the cup to Hrothgar, bidding him be blithe, and afterward to Beowulf and his companions. And she thanked God, most wise in words—*wisfæst wordum*—that she could put her trust in any earl for comfort against crime.[4] He partook of the cup, and in reply said that he was resolved to perform deeds of noble valor against the monster, or, if he could not subdue him, to await his last days in the meadhall. And the poem further relates that—

"The woman liked the Goth's proud speech right well;
His boasting pleased the joyful people's queen;
Then she, gold-decked, went by her lord to sit."[5]

These glimpses of a bygone order of things are valuable. They resuscitate the past. We see the men and women

[1] Thorpe, *Northern Mythology*, p. 113.
[2] Polydore Vergil, *History of England*, b. iii., p. 113.
[3] Thorpe's Beowulf, ll., 4040, *et seq.* [4] *Ibid*, p. 42.
[5] Thâm wife tha word wel licodon,
gilp-cwide Geates; eóde gold-hroden,
freólicu folc-cwén, to hire frean sittan.
Beowulf, ix., 1282, *et seq.*

of those old days move and speak before us. Let us approach the mead-hall and learn more of their ways.

V.—The Mead-Hall.

Not very imposing looks the house. It is one story high. It is built of wood. The use of stones for building purposes is not yet known. So identified is timber with building, that the old English word for the act of building is *timbrian*. We enter; but we look in vain for any of the comforts of a modern dwelling-house. Tapestry hangs upon the walls. That which decorated the hall of Heorot was embroidered in gold : " Gold-varied shone the webs along the walls, many wonder-sights to those that gazed upon them."[1] Painted shields and the implements of war look down upon us. There are no chairs. The luxury of a seat with a back to it is still unthought of.[2] But we find stools and benches.[3] 'If we intend staying for the night, those same benches will be our beds, with a pillow, some fresh straw, and perhaps a bear-skin. Bedclothing was scanty in those days, nor was it much needed; the men were better able to endure excessive cold than excessive heat.[4] The floor is

---

[1] *Beowulf*, xv., 1993, *et seq.*

[2] The word chair is not found in Old English ; it is of Gallic origin.

[3] Petersen thus describes an Old Northern guest-hall : " The hall was an oblong parallelogram, having its two longer sides facing the north and the south, with a door at each end exactly opposite the one to the other ; the door was hung on hinges, and provided with a sort of lock. A row of benches was on each side, the higher of which was the most honorable, and in the middle of which was the high seat of the master or chief, having his face toward the north. On the opposite or lower bench was a somewhat lower high seat, exactly opposite the chief's, for the noblest guest."—*Danmark i Hedenhold.* Apud Thorpe, Preface to *Beowulf*, x.

[4] Tacitus, *Germania*, cap. vi.

covered with straw. Indeed, in the Old English way of thinking, to strew is to straw. The words are identical.¹ The table is made of plain boards, pieced together in such a manner that they can afterward be removed.² It was called a *bórd*.³ At an early day the round table was used. It afterward became the custom that each guest had a small side-table; but it was not permitted to eat alone. One of the greatest blots on a man's character would be the fact that he dined in private.⁴ There are no glass windows in this house into which we have been introduced. We perceive only eye-holes — *eág-thyrl*. The Old English do not yet know the use of glass. At present, the birds can fly through the hall in winter; not only are the eye-holes open, but the doors as well.⁵ The fire burns in the center of the hall; there are no chimneys. Perhaps near by is a large tree whose roots are under the floor, and whose branches

---

¹ So also *streaw* means a bed. See Bosworth.

² The following riddle of the Old English writer, Bishop Tahtwin who lived about A. D. 700, tells how the table was broken up after having been used: "The table, speaking in its own person, says that it is in the habit of feeding people with all sorts of viands; that while so doing it is a quadruped, and is adorned with handsome clothing; that afterward it is robbed of all its apparel, and when it has been thus robbed it loses its legs:

'Multiferis omnes dapibus saturare solesco,
Quadrupedem hinc felix ditem me sanxerit ætas,
Esse tamen pulchris fatim dum vestibus ornor,
Certatim me prædones spoliare solescunt ;
Raptis nudate exuviis mox membra relinquunt.'"

MS. *Reg.*, 12th C., xxiii. Apud Wright, *Homes of Other Days*.

³ Whence our words board, boarding, and the like. The original of our table—*tæfl*—was confined to the gaming-table. *Tæflung* meant playing at dice.

⁴ Wright's *Domestic Manners and Sentiments*, p. 19.

⁵ Beda, *Ecclesiastical History*, b. ii., chap. xiii.

cover the roof.¹ In a prominent place is the boar's head in honor of Frey.² The host occupies the highest seat, at about the middle of the table. Near him sits his wife. Upon the table are cheese, and bread, and cereals, and broth, and meat, boiled or roasted.³ The meat is generally salt. Pork was a favorite dish. A servant holds the spit while each guest cuts from it a piece to suit himself. The use of forks is still unknown. Near the fire are ranged the vessels containing the beer. The beer-horn is first handed to the host across the fire. He drinks first. Then all goes merrily. Conversation flows freely. Many are lovers of social converse, haughty warriors. In pleasant cities they sit at the feast and recount tales; then wine wets the man's breast-passions; suddenly rises clamor in the company, and a various outcry is sent forth.⁴ The host makes it a point of honor to quell all disputes. At intervals the harper plays his harp. He is also a poet. He sings the soothing lay, the song serene. He recounts the tales of old. He tells of battles fought and victories won. And, as the wine or beer begins to warm the breasts of the hardy warriors who listen to his lay, they feel the spirit of war rise within them, and in fancy they fight their battles over again. Then they talk of their deeds of prowess, of their hairbreadth escapes; they laugh over their cruelties; they rejoice in their wounds; for, to their thinking, he who had received no wounds knew not the glory of living. From the life we have traced, we can infer the kind of

¹ Müller, *Sagabibliothek*, ii., Saga Völsungs.
² Kemble, *Anglo-Saxons*, vol. i., p. 357.
³ "They had neither green crops nor cultivated fruits. The white crop alone engaged their attention." Guest, *Transactions Philological Society*, May 7, 1852, vol. v., no. 122. A scholarly and valuable paper.
⁴ *Exeter Book*, p. 314.

poetry most in harmony with its sentiments. Let us examine the pieces that have escaped the ravages of time.

VI.—LANGUAGE AND POETRY.

But first a word upon the language. It is the same in which we now write. If it sounds differently, if it requires a special study to understand it, it is because English is a living language, and has received new modes of expression, changed the pronunciation of old words, and, in consequence, their spelling; for it has followed the law of language laid down by Max Müller, in its twofold phase of phonetic decay and dialectical regeneration.[1] But Lappenberg tells us that, of the old language, "about a fifth only is to be pronounced obsolete in the present English."[2] In its use of particles the Old English resembled the Greek.[3] It also had, like the same language, a certain facility of making new compounds. This facility it has mostly lost. It seems to have been transferred to its sister dialect, the German. The Old English mind possessed but a small share of philosophic acuteness. It saw the surface well enough, and what it saw it expressed without circumlocution. Language, in a more civilized condition of life, seeks to veil certain ideas in less offensive words. There is no attempt of this kind among the Old English. They speak as they think; and they think in the concrete. There are no abstractions, no generalizations, no metaphysical terminologies. Every word is uttered with an individualizing force. It stands for a thing. There is

---

[1] *Science of Language*, vol. i., p. 51.
[2] *England under the Anglo-Saxon Kings*, vol. ii., p. 306.
[3] We find traces of a dual form, as in the Greek and Sanskrit, in the pronouns *gyt*, ye two, gen. *incer*, dat. ac. *inc*, you two; and *wyt*, gen. *uncer*, dat. ac. *unc*, we two.

a certain bluntness about the language. It has no power of insinuation; it is not the language of address; it would never have become the vehicle of diplomacy. It moves in a narrow circle of thought. The material, the finite, the tangible, it has words for; the spiritual it can only approximate in the expression of. Such a mind, using such a language, will not be prolific in works of a philosophical character. It will make reflex acts with difficulty; it will not adequately express the sentiments of the heart. It will, properly enough, express emotion, courage, the impulses of nature, action.

1. We possess four precious relics of those Old English days that give us glimpses of the literary spirit of the people who then lived. It has already been seen that no festival was complete without the gleeman and his harp. He traveled far and wide. He was everywhere received with consideration. And one gleeman, who calls himself WIDSITH (*cir.* 370), after passing through various lands, returned to his home and settled down upon his paternal estates. There he recorded his experience, told where he was, and how he was received, together with his friend Scilling. It is thus we possess *The Scóp, or Gleeman's Tale*.[1] The author was well liked. Often had he received a memorable present.[2] "And," he says, "I was with Eormanric a whole season. The king of the Goths well cared for me. He—chief of the burgh-dwellers—gave me a ring for which six hundred sceats of gold were scored, by shillings reckoned; and this I gave to Eadgils—my beloved—when I came home, to repay my friend—prince of the Myrgings—for

[1] *Anglo-Saxon Poems of Beowulf, The Scóp, or Gleeman's Song, and The Fight at Finnesburgh:* Ed. B. Thorpe, London, 1875.
[2] *The Scóp*, ii., 6, 7.

as much as he gave me land, my father's heritage. And another ring gave Ealhhild—noble queen of lords, Eadwine's daughter—and her praise I spread through many lands, and told in song, where under heaven I knew a most excellent gold-adorned queen, gifts dispensing."[1] Thus did he extend the praises of his benefactors. His choicest words were for those who were most generous. He takes pride in telling us that when to the harp his voice resounded, many high-born men, who well knew, said they had never heard better song.[2] Finally, he concludes with a burst of praise upon the standing of the bard with every generous prince :

> "Thus North and South, where'er they roam,
> The sons of song still find a home,
> Speak unreproved their wants, and raise
> Their grateful lay of thanks and praise;
> For still the chief, who seeks to grace
> By fairest fame his pride of place,
> Withholds not from the sacred Bard
> His well-earned praise and high reward;
> But free of hand, and large of soul,
> Where'er extends his wide control,
> Unnumbered gifts his princely love proclaim,
> Unnumbered voices raise to heaven his princely name."[3]

2. Another poem of pre-insular date is the *Lament of Deor*. DEOR is a gleeman or scald who lost his retainership. A rival was given his place. The poet consoles himself in this poem. Others suffered misfortunes and survived them, and why may not he? This is the burden of his song. Indeed, Deor seems to be a man on whom troubles would sit lightly. He was dis-

---

[1] *Ibid*, 177–206.   [2] *Ibid*, 207, *et seq.*
[3] Conybeare's translation in *Illustrations of Anglo-Saxon Poetry.* In this book the translations are made with spirit and fidelity.

posed to look upon the bright side of life. He was, moreover, an independent character. He evidently would not scruple to say disagreeable things. And no doubt it was the asserting of his independence of spirit, and the expression of some offensive remarks, that led his chief to put another in his place. He is silent about the cause. Were chief or rival in fault we would hear it. However, his poem is remarkable as the only one in regular strophic cast that has survived in Old English literature, though many other such there must have been. For this reason, we give our extracts from it in the original, with Thorpe's literal version :

Weland him be wurman	Weland in himself the worm
Wraeces cunnade,	Of exile proved,
Anhydig eorl	The firm-souled chief
Earfotha dreag,	Hardships endured,
Haefde him to gesiththe	Had for his company
Sorge and longath,	Sorrow and weariness,
Winter-cealde wraece,	Winter-cold exile,
Wean oft onfond,	Affliction often suffered,
Siththan hine Nithhad on	When that on him Nithhad
Nede legde,	Constraint had laid,
Swoncre scono bende,	With a tough sinew-band,
Onsyllan mon.	Th' unhappy man.
Thaes ofereode,	That he surmounted,
Thisses swa maeg.	So may I this.

. . . .

We thaet Maethhilde	That of Maethhilde we
Monge gefrugnon :	May have heard :
Wurdon grundlease	Were unreasonable
Geates frige,	Geat's courtships,
The hi seo sorg-lufu	So that from him hapless love
Slaep ealle binom.	All sleep took.
Thaes ofereode,	That he surmounted,
Thisses swa maeg.	So may I this.

. . . .

We geascodan	We have heard tell
Eormanrices	Of Eormanric's
Wylfenne gethoht;	Wolf-like soul;
Ahte wide folc	He owned the ample nation
Gotena rices	Of the Goth's realm;
Tha waes grim cyning	That was a fierce king.
Saet secg monig	Sat many a warrior
Sorgum gebunden	With sorrow bound,
Wean on wenan	Calamity in expectation;
Wyscte genahhe	Wished enough
Tha thæs cyne-rices	That of that kingdom
Ofer cumen wære.	There were an end.
Thæs ofereode	That he surmounted,
Thisses swa mæg.[1]	So may I this.

The poem has allusions to mythic personages, like Weland, or historic beings living in the dim past, like Maethhilde. Eormanric we have found among the friends of the gleeman Widsith. And now let us glance at the themes sung by these poets. Here is one:

3. A very ancient fragment of Continental song among the Old English is *The Fight at Finnesburgh*.[2] Fin, the Frisian prince, is awakened by the glare of the light caused by the firing of his palace by the Danish invaders. The poet is in sympathy with the scene. He contrasts, with no small degree of poetic art, the stillness of the night with the woful deeds caused by the hatred of the people:

> "Sweetly sang the birds of night,
>   The wakeful cricket chirruped loud;
> And now the moon, serenely bright,
>   Was seen beneath the wandering cloud,
> Then roused him swift the deadly foe,
> To deeds of slaughter and of woe.

[1] *Exeter Book*, p. 377.
[2] Text: B. Thorpe's *Beowulf*, etc.

"Now, beneath the ja[...]
The buckler's mass[...]
Anon the chains of sl[...]
That chieftain grea[...]
He whose high prais[...]
First in valor as in [...]
The matchless Hengi[...]

Fin cries to the warrior[s]
hold your ground; be mind[...]
van; fight as one man!"[...]
between themselves and the [...]
encourages the other. In t[...]
of those encouraging speech[...]
cycle of the eighth century[...]
King Theodoric and his me[n]
George Stephens, of Copenh[...]
between two friends in fig[...]
let not thy courage fail thee [...]
when thou art doomed to [...]
shalt have power among me[n]
I never say, my friend, that [...]
play, through fear of any [...]
flee to fortress thy body to [...]
thy mail-shirt hew with bi[...]
sought to fight beyond th[...]
doubt, had we the whole of [...]
many such, but as it stands i[...]

"Through hall did sound the [...]
The shield they could not gr[...]
The floor resounded till fell [...]
Though not alone—fell also [...]

[1] Conybeare's translati[on]
[2] II, 18, *et seq.*
[3] "Mark over border" [...]

OF **CALIFORNIA LIBRARY**

"Now, beneath the javelin's stroke,
　　The buckler's massy circle rung.
Anon the chains of slumber broke:
　　That chieftain great and good,
He whose high praise fills every tongue,
　　First in valor as in blood,
The matchless Hengist to the battle woke."[1]

Fin cries to the warriors: "Awake, my warriors! hold your ground; be mindful of valor; fight in the van; fight as one man!"[2] And, after words passed between themselves and the invaders, they fight. Each encourages the other. In this fragment we have none of those encouraging speeches, but in two leaves of a cycle of the eighth century, treating of the deeds of King Theodoric and his men, lately discovered by Mr. George Stephens, of Copenhagen, we find such a speech between two friends in fight: "Ætla's van-warrior! let not thy courage fail thee to-day, for the day is come when thou art doomed to lose thy life, or thou long shalt have power among men. O Ælfhere's son! may I never say, my friend, that I saw thee at the sword-play, through fear of any man, decline the combat, or flee to fortress thy body to defend, although many foes thy mail-shirt hew with bills, but rather that thou sought to fight beyond the limits of valor."[3] No doubt, had we the whole of this poem, we would find many such, but as it stands it simply describes the fight:

"Through hall did sound the din of slaughter-stroke,
The shield they could not grasp—the bone-helm lacked,
The floor resounded till fell Garulf dead,
Though not alone—fell also many foes;

[1] Conybeare's translation, p. 179.
[2] ll., 18, *et seq.*
[3] "Mark over border" is the original expression.

The raven wheeled above, swart, sallow-brown;
The sword-gleam flashed."

They fought five days. Never heard the poet that sixty conquering heroes behaved so well. Never did song requite as Hnaef requited his young warriors:

"Then sought the vanquished train relief,
And safety for their wounded chief."

The Fight at Finnesburgh was a special favorite with the Old English. When great rejoicings fill the hall of Hrothgar, after Beowulf has killed the fell monster, Grendel, no more popular song can be sung for the occasion than that of Finnesburgh. But who is Beowulf?

4. The grandest monument of Old English poetry we possess is the poem of *Beowulf*.[1] It is an epic dictated by the feelings and thoughts of "the days of yore." Those were times when personality was all; the hero counted for everything. There were no systems; no institutions for leveling up or leveling down the masses; no theory of equality; no scientific, religious, or literary proselytism. Personal energy was the lever upon which men raised themselves above their companions; and that energy was all exercised in the direction of skill in war and the performance of feats of valor and prowess. A hero according to the Old English heart is Beowulf. Hrothgar builds a hall—of halls the greatest—and gives it the name of Heorot. Therein are held feastings and rejoicings; the gleeman sings; treasures are dispensed and presents made. But a grim and

---

[1] Text: T. Arnold, *Beowulf, a Heroic Poem of the Eighth Century*, London, 1876; B. Thorpe, *Anglo-Saxon Poems of Beowulf*, etc., London, 1875.

greedy being who haunts the moors, the fen and fastness, is envious of such joy. He is called Grendel. He enters the hall when the earls have retired to rest; rugged and fierce, he takes thirty of their number; and in his prey exulting goes to his home. Then was there much sorrow in Heorot. During twelve winters' tide did Hrothgar endure the frequent incursions of this foul fiend, till his land was despoiled of its best men, and empty stood the greatest of houses. Then was it noised abroad how Grendel waged war against this good prince and made havoc in his peaceful dominions. It came to the ears of Beowulf. He sets out with his companions to conquer the fiend. He is received with great rejoicings by Hrothgar and his queen. Night comes and the men seek their beds. When all is still, Grendel arrives. There had arisen in him hope of a dainty glut. And first he takes a sleeping warrior, bites his bone-casings —his skin and flesh—drinks his blood; and having devoured him feet and hands, he takes hold of Beowulf. But soon he discovers that he has never encountered a stronger hand-grip; he grows sore afraid, and would fain return to his haunt; but the hero holds him:

> "These warders strong waxed wrathful, fiercer grew,
> The hall resounded; wonder much there was
> That it so well withstood the warring beasts—
> That fell not to the earth this fair land-house.
>
> . . . .
>
> And then arose strange sound; upon the Danes
> Dire terror stood, of all who heard the whoop—
> The horrid lay of God's denier,
> The song that sang defeat and pain bewailed—
> Hell's captive's lay—for in his grasp too firm
> Did he, of men the strongest, hold his prey." [1]

[1] *Beowulf*, xi., 1543-1585.

The noise arouses the men; they take their swords; but no weapon has effect upon this monster. Still in his efforts to get away his sinews spring asunder; the bone-casings burst; he leaves his hand, and death-sick flees to his joyless dwelling; for he knows that his days are numbered. Next day were great rejoicings in Heorot. Thus ends the first encounter of Beowulf.

We learn nothing of the shape, or size, or nature of this mysterious being. That is one of the characteristics of the Old English mind—and one it shares in common with all the Teutonic tribes—that it delights in the mysterious, the undefined, the horrible. In this respect it contrasts with the Greek intellect. Only the sensuous, the palpable, the thing of definite form and beauty, has for it any attraction. Its education is a constant struggle to bridge over all mystery, to cover all deformity, to give everything a name of good omen, to see but the sunshine of life. Homer describes Menelaus as wounded. He forgets the pain and anguish to compare the limbs of Menelaus, stained with gore, to the ivory tinged with purple. The image is too much in accordance with his thoughts to drop it immediately; he tells how the Carian woman lets it lie in her chamber, an object of desire to many a charioteer; but it is intended as an ornament for the king alone, a decoration to the steed and a glory to the rider.[1] The Greek did not live in a land of mist and fog, of marsh and fen and dense forest. He had the sunshine in all its brilliancy; he had a bright atmosphere and clear-cut landscape; therefore his eye was educated to color. With the Old English it was different. In *Beowulf*, the man, the monster, the deed performed are all before us; but

[1] Iliad, ii., 140, *et seq.*

the distinct coloring, the picturesque detail, had no existence, even in the mind of the poet.

The labors of Beowulf are not yet ended. Grendel has a monster-mother, who is bound to be revenged. This is a repetition of the northern conception of "the devil and his dam." She comes the night following and bears away the king's chief counselor. In sorrow the king, his retainers, and Beowulf go to the pool which they know to be her residence. The flood boiled with blood; the folk surveyed the hot gore; the horn sang a death-song. Beowulf plunges in; the ocean surge received the battle warrior; it was a day's space ere he could perceive the ground-plain. Forthwith the she-monster descried him, seized him in her horrid clutches, and to her dwelling bore the prince of rings. He aimed a powerful stroke at her with his war-bill, so that on her head the sword sang a horrid war-song. Then found he that the war-beam would not bite, and in sore straits was he; but trusting in his strength he drags the fiend to the floor; again she overthrows him; but rescuing himself from her, he perceives an old Eotenish sword, the pride of warriors, the work of giants. This he wields and angrily strikes, so that it grips her neck, breaks her bone-rings, and passes through her fated body. On the ground she sank. Beowulf was once more triumphant. Heorot was again secure. Joy reigned; the gleeman's song was heard; the bowl went round; presents were dispensed.

Here the poem naturally ends. But the poet connects with the name of Beowulf another epic cycle as old as the Aryan race. It is that of the dragon. It is found in Grecian and Roman as well as in Teutonic sagas.[1] It is especially an English favorite. We have

[1] The golden fleece is guarded by dragons. A dragon brood kill

here one form of it; but a form more popular still will be that known as St. George and the dragon. Into the present version the poet weaves contemporary and historical allusions and occurrences.[1] But the portions treating of the dragon's depredations and his slaying are remnants of the older saga. For three hundred years had the dragon guarded his treasures unmolested. At last they are discovered and some of them stolen. The hoard-ward's wrath is aroused. No longer would he abide within his mound; but forth he sallied, burning all before him. Nothing living would the hostile airflier leave in his hate to men.[2] The land-dwellers he enveloped in fire and burning. Beowulf resolves to destroy him single-handed. "The prince of rings disdained to seek the wide-flier with a numerous band; he dreaded not the conflict."[3] Arming himself, with a few trusty comrades he seeks the dragon's haunt:

> "Firm rose the stone-wrought vault, a living stream
> Burst from the barrow, red with ceaseless flame
> That torrent glowed; nor lived there soul of man
> Might tempt the dread abyss, nor feel its rage.
> So watched the fire-drake o'er his hoard—and now
> Deep from his laboring breast the indignant Goth
> Gave utterance to the war-cry. Loud and clear
> Beneath the hoar stone rung the deafening sound,
> And strife uprose: the watcher of the gold
> Had marked the voice of man. First from his lair,
> Shaking firm earth, and vomiting, as he strode,
> A foul and fiery blast, the monster came.
> Yet stood beneath the barrow's lofty side

Oftnitt in the *Heldenbuch*. Martial compares a miser to a dragon guarding its hoard. (Lib. 12, ep. 45.)

[1] Cantos xxxiv., xxxv. This has misled Mr. T. Arnold and others as to the real antiquity of the poem.

[2] xxxiii., l., 4620., Thorpe's edition.   [3] 4680.

> The Goth's unshaken champion, and opposed
> To that infuriate foe his full-orbed shield.
> Then the good war-king bared his trenchant blade:
> Tried was its edge of old, the stranger's dread,
> And keen to work the foul aggressor's woe.
>
> . . . .
>
> The kingly Goth
> Reared high his hand, and smote the grisly foe,
> But the dark steel upon the unyielding mail
> Fell impotent, nor served its master's need
> Now at his utmost peril. Nor less that stroke
> To maddening mood the barrow's warder roused:
> Outburst the flame of strife, the blaze of war
> Beamed horribly; still no triumph won the Goth,
> Still failed his keen brand in the unequal fray. . . .
> Again they met—again with freshened strength
> Forth from his breast the unconquered monster poured
> That pestilent breath. Encompassed by its flames,
> Sad jeopardy and new the chieftain held."[1]

But with the assistance of Wiglaf, his trusty companion, he succeeds in killing the monster, and soon after dies of the poisoned wounds he has received. "No sound of harp shall the warrior awake; but the dusky raven ready o'er the fallen shall speak many things—to the eagle shall tell how he fared at his food while with the wolf he spoiled the slain."[2] Such is the lament made over the dead hero.

The version of this poem now known is not that sung on the seashore and in the primeval forests of the Continental homestead. It is a more modern version. The unknown bard that wrote it was a Christian. None other could have spoken of Cain; none other would have called the people heathens; none other would have said

[1] Conybeare's translation, *Illustrations of Anglo-Saxon Poetry*, p. 69.
[2] xli., 6041.

that they knew not the Creator.[1] He was in all probability a monk. No one else could scarcely attempt to preach after this fashion : "Woe to him who shall through cruel malice thrust a soul into the fire's embrace ; let him not look for comfort."[2] No one else would lay down so nicely the doctrine of repentance as he does in these words : "It was no longer than one night when he committed more murders, and mourned not for his enmity and crime ; he was too confirmed in them."[3] He also has glimpses of true poetry : here is a genuine beam :

"When sorrow on him came, and pain befell,
He left the joy of men and chose God's light."[4]

But who this poet-soul was, we know not ; when he lived we can only conjecture. That he wrote this version of *Beowulf* after Cedmon[5] had sung of the creation is certain ; for to his poem he alludes in unmistakable language when he represents the gleeman singing of the origin of things : how the Almighty wrought the earth ; how he set the sun and moon to give light to those dwelling on land ; how he created plant and animal.[6] There are many theories concerning the poem. Thorpe considers it "a metrical paraphrase of an heroic saga, composed in the southwest of Sweden, in the old common language of the North, and probably brought to this country during the sway of the Danish dynasty.'[7] Haigh rejects Thorpe's view, considers the poem en-

[1] *Beowulf,* ii., 860, *et seq.*
[2] *Ibid.*
[3] ii., 273-5.
[4] He thá mid tháere sorge ; thá him sió sár belamp,
   gum-dreám ofgeaf ; Godes leoht geceás.—xxxv., 4928-32.
[5] A. D. 670.   [6] I., 180-198.   [7] *Beowulf,* Preface, ix.

tirely English, both in scenes, incidents, and personages, and believes it to have been composed in England.¹ Henry Morley is disposed to follow him. He says he is almost tempted to make Bowlby Cliff the ness on which Beowulf was buried; "Bowlby then being read as the corrupted form of Beowulfes-by."² Kemble was at first inclined to regard the poem as historical, and so expressed himself in the preface to the text which he published in 1833. But in the preface to his translation issued in 1837, he announced an entirely new theory. With Grimm, he regards it as mythic. He finds that the old Saxons called their harvest-month Beo or Bewod, after the god of fertility. This god he identifies with Beowulf. The poem will not bear out the supposition. It deals with historical personages. Some of them can be identified with well-known records. Thus, Hygelac is spoken of by Gregory of Tours, under the Frankish form of Chochilaic, just as Hûlfreich is called Chilperic.³ According to Thorkelin, Beowulf was a living personage also. He assigns, upon authority other than his own, the year of his death as A. D. 340. Now, the name of Beowulf must have been popular in song and story; and as it receded in the past, to the deeds of valor of which its bearer was the author were added others of a marvelous and mysterious character. Traditions of time immemorial were strung upon it; these were sung in the old homestead; they were remembered

¹ *The Anglo-Saxon Sagas.* This is also the opinion of Mr. T. Arnold. He considers it a West-Saxon poem of the eighth century.

² *A First Sketch of English Literature,* p. 14.

³ His gestis Dani cum rege suo, nomine Chochilaicho, evectu navali per mare Gallias appetunt. III., 8. It may be remarked with Ettmüller that all the Northern pirates were sometimes called Danes. See Thorpe, *Int.,* xxv.

in the new; but the scenes of the ancestral home becoming effaced from memory, men sought in the new country to give them "a local habitation and a name." Never seeing the ness upon which the hero was buried, and a mound erected to his honor, they are only following their instincts in designating a place to which they transfer the interest vested in the old scenes. As the poem passes down from mouth to mouth, the descriptions become changed to suit the newly designated places. Such, in our opinion, was the fate of *Beowulf*. When the Danish dynasty held sway, such a poem was calculated to be recited with renewed interest, and at this time we conceive it to have received its present form.[1]

In the poem of *Beowulf*, especially in those parts of it savoring of the old Continental homestead, we find an absence of a spiritual and a spiritualizing ideal. Physical prowess is personified in the hero. The people are hero-worshipers. The assistance of God alluded to is an afterthought improvised by the Christian poet. No visible intervention of supernatural powers fills the narrative, as in Homer; no sentiment of chivalry or love; but the seeking of a mere selfish glory. Brute force is the ideal; Beowulf is the war-beast. It is the poem of a people living to war, glorying in battle, and dying to renew their fights and repeat their deeds of valor within the halls of Valhalla.

VII.—Philosophy.

Such is the literature of the Old English. And now we come to their philosophy. Let it not be said that they possessed none. There is no people without a philosophy, for all have reason, and all ask the why

[1] Thorpe considers the only MS. extant (MS. Cott. Vitellius, A. 15), "to be of the first half of the eleventh century."—*Beowulf*, Preface, xi.

and wherefore of things. Whence came I? who made this earth? these stars? the seasons? the heat and the cold? the winds and the rain, and the refreshing springs and cooling streams? These are questions that occur to the most primitive people. And sometimes they even reflect on the more difficult issues of life and death. They ask: Why am I here? what is the motive of life? who guides, directs the actions of men? Are they the result of chance, or is there order in events? The Old English reflected on all these questions, and had their answers for them. Their sagas, and still more their mythology, are so many efforts to solve these ever-recurring thoughts. They themselves may not have suggested the solutions; in all probability they did not; from other and more distant sources did they come. They are to be found in the Scandinavian mythology of the Edda. Composed by a people who abandoned their country and sought in the cold regions of Iceland a home in which they might cling to their traditions and their gods, this book is the one certain source whence we can draw their solutions of the world-riddle. It was the common inheritance of the Angle and the Saxon as well as of the Norwegian. Malte Brun recognizes the fact, but accounts for it by supposing that the Scandinavians are descended "from a primitive race, indigenous to the countries which it still inhabits";[1] and that it was this primitive race that peopled the South from the North. The truth is the reverse of this. The first migrations were northward. Those from the North in after-ages were a reaction and a compensation of the primitive migrations. We distinguish two of them. The oldest has left its traces in the traditions of giants and dwarfs, of magical influ-

[1] *Geography*, vol. iii., bk. cxlvii., p. 1038.

ence and communication with evil spirits. The later is that distinctly recorded by Snorri Sturleson in the Prose Edda. While the local coloring and specific naming are his, the tradition is substantially that believed by his forefathers. He tells us : " Othin had spædom, and so also his wife ; and from this knowledge found he out that his name would be held high in the north part of the world, and worshiped beyond all kings ; for this sake was he eager to go on his way from Tyrkland. . . . But whithersoever they fared over the land, much fame was said of them, so that they were thought to be liker gods than men, and they stayed not their faring till they came northward into that land that is now called Saxland ;[1] there dwelt Othin a long time, and had that land far and wide for his own. . . . These Asa took to them wives there within the land, but some for their sons, and these races waxed full many ; so that about Saxland, and all thence about the north country they spread, so that the tongue of the Asiamen was the true tongue over all these lands ; and men deem from the way that the names of these forefathers are written, that these names have belonged to this tongue, and the Asa brought the tongue hither into the north country: into Norway, into Svithiod, into Denmark, and into Saxland. . . ."[2] One fact underlies this remarkable passage, and it is all we are concerned with at present, that the mythology of the Æsir was universal throughout the Teutonic nations. Let us see how they questioned and how they answered on the great problems of life, creation, and thought.

[1] The whole of Germany was frequently known by the old writers as Saxland.
[2] *Foreword to the Edda.* Translation of G. W. Dasent, pp. 109–111. Stockholm, 1842.

They contemplated the heavens and the earth, and they wished to account for their existence. This question they solved on the same principle on which the Chaldeans of old had solved it. The Chaldean found, in two primary elements, the igneus and the humid, the source of all things; from their union did he conceive all things to spring.[1] The Old English imagined all things also to spring from the union of heat and cold. We are told that from Niflheim,[2] the home of mist, issued cold, and from Muspellzheim, the home of fire, issued heat. The heat melted the ice; the drops formed thereby, through His power who sent forth the heat, received life, and a being, called Ymir, was produced. We are further told that while Ymir slept, offspring came forth from him.[3] This account of the origin of man nearly coincides with the Hindu, which represents the various classes as springing respectively from the heads, the arms, the thighs, and the feet of Brahma.[4] But there is a difference. Brahma is the Author of all things, while back of Ymir seems to be a Creator. In fact, Ymir is the primeval chaos. His other name is Aurgelmir.[5]

> "When Ymir lived
> Was sand, nor sea,
> Nor cooling wave;
> No earth was found,
> Nor heaven above;
> One chaos all,
> And nowhere grass."[6]

---

[1] Lenormant, *Legend of Semiramis*, p. 62.
[2] Nefl—νεφελη—nebula.
[3] Thorpe, *Northern Mythology*, vol. I., p. 3.
[4] *Manavadharmasastra.*
[5] Aur—matter, mud, clay.
[6] *Völuspá.*

So we are further told that Bör's sons, having slain Ymir, carried his body to Ginnunga-gap—the yawning gap or the abyss of pure space—and formed of it the earth; of his blood they made the sea and fresh waters; of his bones the mountains; of his teeth and grinders and those bones that were broken, they made stones and pebbles; in the great impassable ocean, formed of the blood that flowed from his wounds, they set the earth around which it circles; of his skull they formed the heavens, which they set up over the earth with four regions, and under each corner placed a dwarf, the names of whom were Austri, Vestri, Northri, and Southri—the four points of the compass; of his brain they formed the heavy clouds; of his hair the vegetable creation; and of his eyebrows a wall of defense against the giants; this they placed round Midgard, the midmost part of the earth, the dwelling-place of the sons of men.[1] In this manner, the saga goes on to say how sun and moon and stars received their proper places in Nature, and how the days and the years came to be reckoned. In this first lisping of philosophy the problems of time and space are considered. The heavenly origin of things is kept in view; knowledge comes from above. But there is a principle of evil in things of earth; for Ymir, the shapeless mass out of whom hill and dale, river and ocean were framed, "was evil, together with all his race."[2] And this evil race dwelt in Jötenheim. They were giants and the sworn enemies of the Æsir. When Ymir was killed all the giants were drowned, save Bergelmir and his wife, who escaped in a chest, and thus continued the hateful race.

[1] *Völuspá*; see also Thorpe, *Northern Mythology*, vol. i., p. 5.
[2] Thorpe, *Northern Mythology*, p. 8.

Is there not here a clear reminiscence of the Deluge recorded in the Bible?

And there is another fact recorded in that Book which was not forgotten by these peoples of the North. We are told therein that in the garden of Paradise stood a certain tree on which depended the life and death, the happiness and misery, of the human race. In the mythology of the North is it also set down concerning a tree of life. It was called Yggdrasil. It was "a stately tree, with white dust strewed: thence came the dews that wet the dales; it stands, ever green, over Urda's well."[1] Beneath the roots of the Yggdrasil, by the well of Urd, there stands a fair hall, whence go forth three maidens, Urd, Verdandi, and Skuld. They are called Norns. They engrave on the tablet of time; they determine the lives of men; they fix their destinies. In modern language these maidens are known as Past, Present, and Future. They are the molders of man's destiny. Life itself is ever green, ever fresh, ever flowing; but time is all the same, determining each individual's course. This idea of a fate influencing men, decreeing their deaths, and shaping their lives, was deeply implanted in the Teutonic mind. There are the Valkyriur. They are ever in attendance upon Odin. Prior to a battle they come from afar to sway the victory[2] and choose those who are to fall and dwell in Valhalla. In the myth of Frey and Gerd, Skimen sings: "My life was decreed to one day only, and my days are determined by fate."[3] The Christian poet who revised the poem of *Beowulf* was not able to rid himself of this philosophy as well as he did of the mention of the heathen gods. Thus, the hero says: Fate goes ever as it

---

[1] Sæmunda's Edda, *Völuspá*.   [2] *Völuspá*.
[3] Thorpe, *Northern Mythology*, vol. i., p. 47.

must—*gaeth á wyrd swá hió sceal.*[1] But already it is coupled in the poet's mind with the idea of direfulness; he speaks of it as a grim power—*geósceaf grimne.*[2] His ancestors would not have so qualified it. For them it possessed nothing grim or dreadful. Death in fight was their joy and the ideal termination of life. Old age was not a coveted boon:

> "The coward thinks to live for ever,
> If he avoid the weapon's reach;
> But age, which overtakes at last,
> Twines his gray hair with pain and shame."[3]

The growth of plant and animal was another problem contemplated by these peoples. Everything living and active was endowed with a personality. Nicors inhabited the running stream. Tree and plant were the dwelling of the genius that made them grow. Nature was a vast laboratory in which inert matter was transformed into vegetable and animal life by a personal being. Dwarfs were the instruments by which many changes were brought about. They had charge of the gold and precious stones concealed in the bowels of the earth. The echoes in the mountains were the answers of the dwarfs.[4] The creation of man these peoples conceived to have been the work of three of their gods. The saga tells us that Odin, Hænir, and Lodur, meeting the ash and the elm, changed the one into a man and

---

[1] *Beowulf*, vi., 915.
[2] xviii., 2472.
[3] Sæmunda's Edda, *Hava-Mal*, tr. W. Taylor. So, too, *Beowulf*, xxi., 2781-3.
[4] Grimm, *Deutsch. Myth.*, 421, O. N. Dvergmál. So, rock-crystal was known as dwarf-stone, *dvœrg sten*, and in Denmark certain stones are still called dwarf-hammers. See Thorpe, *Northern Mythology*, vol. i., p. 8.

the other into a woman. And Odin gave them soul; Hœnir, mind; Lodur, blood. The ash is henceforth known as the life-tree.[1] Thus did these simple peoples distinguish between the material and spiritual elements in man, although they never defined what was matter and what spirit. Indeed, in spite of the distinction in their mythology, their thoughts became too materialized. But there is one passage in *Beowulf* which has the ring of an Old English idea. It asserts the supremacy of the understanding. It is a remarkable expression; for it is one of the very few that anywhere assert the superiority of spirit over matter. "Understanding, deliberation, forethought of mind," says Beowulf, "is everywhere best."[2] This is a thought as old as the Aryan family. In a Hindu book, purporting to give good advice in the guise of fables, it is asserted that knowledge is the fountain-head of all happiness, and by a most illogical process is it shown to be so: "Knowledge gives good behavior; from good behavior one attains worthiness; from being worthy one gets to be wealthy; from wealth one reaches religious merit, afterward happiness."[3] The ideas in both are of a piece with the thoroughly English maxim, "Knowledge is power." That in *Beowulf* reveals the germ of modern English philosophy. The human understanding is the one theme it seems to have fathomed, from the problem of knowing discussed by Locke, to that of the unknowable treated by Herbert Spencer. And that problem, when made the exclusive one of philosophy

[1] *Cwicbeam.* See "A spell to promote the fertility of land," from MS. Cott. Caligula, A. 7, printed in Rask's A. S. Grammar.
[2] xvi., 2123—5.
[3] Vidyâ dadâti vinayam vinayâtyâti pâtratatâm pâtratvaddhanam-âpnoti dhanaddharmam tatah sukham."—*Hitopadesa*, b. i., 6.

and identified with it, has only the same outcome it has had with the Hindu mind; it will end in Nirvana; it will make nihilism the last word of English philosophy.

The question of good and evil was a puzzling one for the Old English mind. It recognized the one and the other. There never was a nation without primary ideas of right and wrong; but the explanation that each people gives varies. To the Teuton, when men were first formed they were happy. But the frost-giants came among them and taught them evil. One especially, called Gullveig,[1] spread avarice and the love of gain among them: and though she was thrice burned, she arose as often from her ashes, and she still lives. She was the first to cause human blood to flow, and the saga tells us that it is because of her decree that it still flows. The suffering of the good and innocent was also a difficult problem for these peoples. Life was not to them what it is to the Christian, a period of probation and meriting; it therefore never entered their minds that misery might be a boon. They cut the Gordian knot by saying that some men fell under the influence of good spirits, and some of evil. Even among their gods they recognized one as actuated by wickedness. He was a spirit of craft and cunning. He was known as Loki, and was the source of innumerable annoyances to gods and men. Still he seemed to have made himself a sort of necessity for them; for when Thor loses his hammer, to Loki he goes to find it for him.[2] Philosophy was for the Northman made up of riddles. Odin undertakes to contend with Vafthrudni in learning. He approaches him in disguise. Vafthrudni tells him:

[1] *i. e.*, gold-matter.   [2] *Thrym's Quida.*

> "Know that to thy parting step
> Never shall these doors unfold,
> If thy tongue excel not mine
> In the strife of mystic lore." [1]

It is a matter of life or death to answer his questions. Thus is knowledge a prize to be struggled for; if needs be, to die for.

Such is the people we have attempted to describe; we have dived into its thoughts; we have measured the beatings of its heart; we have seen how its days were passed in the mist-land of its Continental homesteads; we have contemplated the germs of important modern institutions, but we have noticed very few indications of the great irresistible nation which was in after-times to play such a conspicuous part in molding the civilizations of Europe and America. But who sees the hero in the infant child? Still, this child, under Keltic, Roman, and Christian influences, will wax strong. It will learn new ideas and new modes of life. New sentiments and aptitudes will be infused into it. Let us watch its growth under the fostering care of each influence.

[1] *Vafthrudni's mal.*

CHAPTER II.

KELTIC INFLUENCE.

I.—KELT AND TEUTON.

BOTH Kelt and Teuton started from the same Aryan homestead. They had the same stock of ideas, the same principle of action, the same manners and customs. They spoke the same language with very slight difference. "A wonderful analogy," says Dr. Herman Ebel, speaking of the affinity of conjugations, "with the Teutonic and Slavonian is found to exist, which points to a most special connection of these languages, the result either of long-continued unity, or of a very special relationship of the mind of the peoples."[1] After centuries of separation these kindred peoples meet. They no longer recognize each other. Their forms of speech have diverged. So have their character and disposition. They have retained little in common beyond some laws and customs.

The English, with their ideal of brute force and their superstitious natures, with their love for war and greed

---

[1] *Celtic Studies*, translated by W. K. Sullivan, § 14, p. 127. Dr. Sullivan says, speaking of Gaulish names, "Both Irish and German do and should explain them, for they must have been nearly identical a few centuries before the Christian era."—*Introduction to O'Curry's Manners and Customs of the Ancient Irish*, p. lxxvii.

for plunder, came among their Keltic kinsmen. For centuries they had been slowly but effectively gaining a foothold in the island. As early as A. D. 289 we find Carausius employing large bodies of Frankish mercenaries.[1] In the fifth century their numbers became so great that the conflict was one of life or death. Then it is that the English settlement became a matter of history. But it is erroneous to think that the English ever drove all their Keltic kin into the mountains of Wales.[2] Some they lived among on terms of equality; others they subjugated and attached to the soil. But in the course of ages these latter regained their independence and amalgamated with their conquerors. With Keltic blood, Keltic genius and the Keltic spirit became infused. And this commingling of the two races is more widespread than is generally conceded or than either people is conscious of. About forty years ago W. F. Edwards examined the matter from a physiological standpoint, and came to the conclusion that there was a much larger Keltic element in the present English population than is indicated by names. "Attached to the soil," says he, speaking of the Britons, " they will have shared in that emancipation which, during the course of the middle ages, gradually restored to political life the mass of the population in the countries of Western Europe; recovering by slow degrees their rights without resum-

[1] *Ibid.*, p. xlii.
[2] I am surprised to find so painstaking an historian as Mr. Green, in his delightful *Short History of the English People*, admit this common but erroneous opinion. Creasy is of a different mind. In his *English Constitution*, he states expressly that "the British element was largely preserved in our nation." See also a very able paper in the *Trans. Philological Society*, 1857, p. 39, *On the Connection of the Keltic with the Teutonic Languages, and especially with the Anglo-Saxon*, by the Rev. John Davies, M. A.

ing their name, and rising gradually with the rise of industry, they will have got spread through all ranks of society. The gradualness of this movement, and the obscurity which enwrapped its beginnings, allowed the contempt of the conqueror and the shame of the conquered to become fixed feelings; and so it turns out that an Englishman, who now thinks himself sprung from the Saxons or Normans, is often in reality the descendant of the Britons."[1] Mr. Henry Morley studied the question from a purely literary point of view, and announces as the result of his investigation this somewhat startling conclusion: "The Celts do not form an utterly distinct part of our mixed population. But for the early, frequent, and various contact with the race that in its half-barbarous days invented Oisin's dialogues with St. Patrick, and that quickened afterward the Northmen's blood in France, Germanic England would not have produced a Shakespeare."[2] Mr. Matthew Arnold brought to bear upon the subject his trained critical talent, and gives the result of his study in these words: "If I were asked where English poetry got these three things, its turn for style, its turn for melancholy, and its turn for natural magic, for catching and rendering the charm of nature in a wonderfully near and vivid way, I should answer with some doubt that it got much of its turn of style from a Celtic source; with less doubt, that it got much of its melancholy from a Celtic source; with no doubt at all, that from a Celtic source it got nearly all its natural magic."[3] Thus we find all

---

[1] *Des Caractères Phisiologiques des Races Humaines considérés dans leurs Rapports avec l'Histoire*, quoted in Matthew Arnold's *Celtic Literature*.
[2] *Early English Writers*, vol i., part i., p. 188.
[3] *Celtic Literature*, p. 135.

those who make a careful anatomy of English thought conclude that the Keltic element is a strong influencing agency in determining its present and past preëminence. Let us now see what there is in Keltic character and Keltic thought to exert this great influence.

In character and disposition the Kelt differs from the Teuton. The Kelt is flighty and fickle; the Teuton is sluggish in his movements, but steady and persevering. The nature of the one is more spiritual than that of the other. Its ideal is more elevated. It has greater susceptibility for the beautiful and the sensuous.[1] It lays stress upon color and form. Bright color and beautiful form delight it. The Teutonic nature looks more to the inner view of things. It is not dazzled by show. If it fights, it must be for something more tangible than mere honor or championship; it must be for riches, or power, or conquest, or in defense of person and property. Not so the Keltic disposition. Its valor is for valor's sake. An opinion or a principle is sufficient reason in its sight to fight, and even to die for. The Kelt lacks the steadiness of the Teuton. He is impatient of labor. He would achieve results at a bound. He does not know how to plod. His is an emotional nature. It is easily elevated and as easily depressed. It has not seriousness enough. It is fond of excitement; it glories in appearances.

" For acuteness and valor the Greeks;
For excessive pride the Romans;
For dullness the creeping Saxons;
For beauty and love the Gaedhils."

[1] Distinguish between the *sensuous* and the *sensual*. The sensual refers to that which is gross, material, carnal; the sensuous is that which appeals to the eye, or ear, as rhythm, harmony, color, form. It is in this sense Milton uses the word sensuous in his well-known de-

So speaks an Irish poem, forgetful that the persistency of "the creeping Saxon" is the source of his strength and the secret of his enduring power.

II.—KYMRIC KELT.

When the English and Welsh fought for mastery in the island of Britain, the latter were greatly disorganized. Centuries of struggles had exhausted them. Whatever tinge of Roman civilization they may have acquired, left among them no other trace than the story of Brutus, the grandson of Æneas. This was the sole legacy of pagan Rome. But they were a Christian people. They had their churches, their schools, and their priesthood. They were attached to Rome and its teachings. They recognized the Pope, and referred to him all their difficulties.[1] In all other respects both clergy and people are greatly demoralized. Their private feuds they gratify at the expense of the public good. GILDAS writes in the sixth century.[2] His soul is grieved

scription of poetry, in which he tells us it must be "simple, sensuous, and impassioned."

[1] Gildas, in his epistle (§ 67), complains of those who cross the seas urging their claims to church benefices. That document, first brought to light by Spelman, and printed in Wilkins's *Concilia* (vol. i., p. 28), in which Dinoth writes in Keltic to St. Augustine, that he acknowledges no other obedience "to him whom you call the Pope than that dictated by charity," is now regarded as a forgery. For an exposition of the reasons, see Döllinger's *Church History*—tr. Cox., vol. ii., pp. 61, 62. An ancient British or English Church, not in communion with Rome, is an historical myth.

[2] Works: *Epistola de Excidio Britanniæ et Castigatio Ecclesiastici Ordinis.* This was translated in 1638, under the title *The Epistle of Gildas, the most ancient British author; who flourished in the yeere of our Lord 546. And who by his great erudition, sanctitie, and wisdome, acquired the name of* SAPIENS. *Faithfully translated out of the originall*

and indignant at the state of affairs. He conceals nothing. He tells his countrymen, individually and collectively, their failings : "It has always been a custom with our nation," he writes, "as it is at present, to be impotent in repelling foreign foes, but bold and invincible in raising civil war, and bearing the burden of their offenses ; they are impotent, I say, in following the standard of peace and truth, but bold in wickedness and falsehood."[1] He leaves his unfortunate country, goes to Brittany, and settles in Vannes. Thence he flings his fierce invective against all orders of society. He draws a frightfully vivid picture of men in church and state. He boils with rage against Vortigern for asking the aid of "the fierce and impious Saxons, a race hateful both to God and man."[2] His description of the ravages of this "wolfish offspring" glows with the glare of the fires they kindled : "The fire of vengeance, justly kindled by former crimes, spread from sea to sea, fed by the hands of our foes in the East, and did not cease, until, destroying the neighboring towns and lands, it reached the other side of the island, and dipped its red and savage tongue in the western ocean. . . . Lamentable to behold, in the midst of the streets lay the tops of lofty towers, tumbled to the ground, stones of high walls, holy altars, fragments of human bodies, covered with livid clots of coagulated blood, looking as if they had been squeezed together in a press, and with no chance of being buried, save in the ruins of the

---

Latine. London, 12mo, 1638. Another version, based upon this, is that of Dr. Giles, published in Bohn's Antiquarian Library, in the volume entitled *Six Old English Chronicles*. St. Gildas, according to Geoffrey of Monmouth, translated the Molmutine Laws from the Keltic. (*Hist. Brit.*, lib. ii., cap. 17.)

[1] *Epistola*, § 21. [2] *Ibid*, § 23.

houses, or in the ravening bellies of wild beasts and birds."[1] Even this language pales before the torrent of indignation that fills his soul as he contemplates the moral evils of his people: "Britain has kings, but they are tyrants; she has judges, but unrighteous ones; generally engaged in plunder and rapine, but always preying on the innocent; whenever they exert themselves to avenge or protect, it is sure to be in favor of robbers and criminals; they have an abundance of wives, yet are they addicted to fornication and adultery."[2] . . . Britain hath priests, but they are unwise; very many that minister, but many of them impudent; clerks she hath, but certain of them are deceitful raveners; pastors, so called, but rather wolves prepared for the slaughter of souls (for they provide not for the good of the common people, but covet rather the gluttony of their own bellies); . . . seldom sacrificing, and seldom with clean hearts, standing at the altars.[3] . . ." But why continue? Take the catalogue of all imaginable crimes, condense them into one book through which is infused a burning lava of indignation, and you possess the essence of this Epistle of Gildas. Nor is he content with generalities. He calls upon the leading men by name; he sets them face to face with their crimes; he heaps on their heads the whole responsibility of their country's ruin. "What dost thou, also, thou lion's whelp (as the prophet saith), Aurelius Conanus? Art not thou as the former (if not far more foul) to thy utter destruction, swallowed up in the filthiness of horrible murders, fornications, and adulteries, as by an overwhelming flood of the sea? Hast not thou by hating, as a deadly serpent, the peace of thy country, and thirsting unjustly after civil wars

[1] *Ibid*, § 24. [2] *Ibid*, § 66.
[3] *Ibid*, § 27.

and frequent spoils, shut the gates of heavenly peace and repose against thine own soul?[1] . . . Thou, also, who, like to the spotted leopard, art diverse in manners and in mischief, whose head now is growing gray, who art seated on a throne full of deceits, and from the bottom even to the top art stained with murder and adulteries, thou naughty son of a good king, like Manasses sprung from Ezekiah, Vortipore, thou foolish tyrant of the Demetians, why art thou so stiff?[2] . . ." None but a Briton could speak with such earnestness to his fellow Britons.[3] The impatience, the restlessness, the unconquerable shame at defeat, the inability to make most of one's position, all reveal the Keltic nature.

Among those things for which Gildas reproaches the clergy, is that of being "negligent and dull to listen to the precepts of the holy saints (if ever they did so much as once hear that which full often they ought to hear), but diligent and attentive to the plays and foolish fables of secular men, as if they were the very ways to life, which indeed are but the passages to death."[4] This shows that though independence and virtue—land and goods—might pass from the Kymry, they still retained their love for song and story. Indeed, when Gildas lived was one of the brightest eras of Kymric poetry. His brother Aneurin and his schoolmate Llywarch Hen are the greatest names in the literature of his people. The poet's art was cultivated and cher-

[1] *Ibid*, § 30.   [2] *Ibid*, § 31.
[3] It is strange that Henry Morley should doubt the authenticity of this book, or think of attributing it to other than Gildas. The vehemence of the style and the indignation are all too earnest for any one to assume them without feeling them. His words burn. Both manner and matter point to a Briton as the author, whether that Briton is Gildas or another.
[4] *Ep.*, § 66.

ished by Christian bards with as much assiduity as in Druidical days. The remnants of bardic lore that have come down to us in the precepts and maxims known as Triads, reveal an admirable knowledge of human nature and the laws of composition. They show that a bard's education was a serious affair. His acquisitions were manifold; his criterion of excellence was elevated; his attainments were put to severe tests. Here are the teachings of the Triads:

"The three qualifications of poetry: Endowment of genius, judgment from experience, and happiness of mind.

"The three primary requisites of genius: An eye that can see nature; a heart that can feel nature; and boldness that dares follow it.

"The three foundations of judgment: Bold design, frequent practice, and frequent mistakes.

"The three foundations of learning: Seeing much, suffering much, and studying much.

"The three foundations of happiness: A suffering with contentment, a hope that it will come, and a belief that it will be.

"The three foundations of thought: Perspicuity, amplitude, and justness.

"The three canons of perspicuity: The word that is necessary, the quantity that is necessary, and the manner that is necessary.

"The three canons of amplitude: Appropriate thought, variety of thought, and requisite thought. . . .

"The three duties of a bard: Just composition, just knowlledge, and just criticism."[1]

With principles thus clearly laid down it is to be looked for that this people excel in style. And such we find to be the case. It has great mastery of expression. It has a superabundance of words. Its lively imagina-

[1] Ancient British Triads in *Relics of the Welsh Bards*, by Edward Jones, 1794.

tion, trained and bridled by thorough discipline, employs metaphor and likeness with an ease and grace that we seek in vain among the Old English writers. One of the most spirited odes in Old English is that commemorative of the *Battle of Brunanburh* in 938. In this manner it tells of the flight of the Scottish clans and of the slaughter made among them :

> "Pursuing fell the Scottish clans;
> The men of the fleet in numbers fell;
> Midst the din of the field, the warriors swate.
> . . . .
> No slaughter yet was greater made
> E'er in this island, of people slain,
> Before this same, with the edge of the sword." [1]

Now, compare with this the battle-ode of ANEURIN (510–560). Note the abundance of imagery and the graceful form of expression :

> ' Have ye seen the tusky boar,
> Or the bull with sullen roar,
> On surrounding foes advancing?
> So Garadawg bore his lance.
> . . . .
> As the flame's devouring force,
> As the whirlwind in its course,
> As the thunder's fiery stroke,
> Glancing on the shivered oak;
> Did the sword of Vedel's mow
> The crimson harvest of the foe." [2]

Again, it is only the Kymric bard that truly possesses " an eye that can see nature and a heart that can

[1] Ingram's version in the *Anglo-Saxon Chronicle*.
[2] Gododin, Gray's version, in Jones's *History of Ancient Welsh Bards*, p. 18.

feel nature." Here is an instance of that rare blending of nature into action. TALIESIN (520–570)—Shining Forehead—sings the deeds of Urien. He also is contemporary with Gildas. He is Urien's chief bard. He thus describes Urien's prowess : " Doorkeeper ! listen ! What noise is that ? Is it the earth that shakes ? Or is it the sea that swells, rolling its white head toward thy feet ? Is it above the valley ? It is Urien that thrusts. Is it above the mountains ? It is Urien that conquers. Is it beyond the slope of the hill ? It is Urien who wounds. Is it high in anger ? It is Urien who shouts. Above the road, above the plain, above all the defiles, neither on one side nor on two is there refuge from him."[1] In those days princes and chiefs thought it not beneath them to strike the harp and sing the glories of the land or bewail its misfortunes. Such a bard was LLYWARCH HEN, or the Old (490–580), Prince of Argoed, and companion in arms with Urien. He was devoted to his country, and his sons inherited his spirit. One by one did he see them fall in battle, and lonely and alone he passed through life in his old age, wondering why he should still be left when all that was near and dear to him had passed away.[2] In these touching words he bemoans the loss of his youngest son : "Let the wave break noisily ; let it cover the shore when the joined lances are in battle. O Gwenn ! woe to him who is too old to avenge you ! Let the wave break noisily ; let it cover the plain when the lances join with a shock. . . . Gwenn has been slain at the ford of Morlas. Here is the bier made for him by his fierce-conquered enemy after he had been surrounded on all sides by the army of the Lloegrians ; here is the

[1] Quoted in Henry Morley's *Early Writers*, vol. i., part i.
[2] See his address to his crutch.

tomb of Gwenn, the son of the old Llywarch. *Sweetly a bird sang on a pear-tree above the head of Gwenn, before they covered him with turf: that broke the heart of the old Llywarch.*[1] Here we have the perfect poet soul, brave and generous ; but so tender, so susceptible to every touch of nature. This susceptibility, this tenderness, this sweet melancholy, the English will imbibe to a certain degree from their Welsh kin.

III.—GAEDHIL AND KYMRY.

But the Britons themselves learned some of their artistic cunning from their Gaedhilic brethren. Much of their brightest imagery, many of their most significant legends, came out of the sister isle. "One thing is certain : the traditions that form the basis of Welsh poetry and literature, and many of their laws, are not Welsh, but belong to their earlier conquerors, the Irish, or their later ones, the Strathclyde Britons."[1] In the Gaedhilic poetry we find great accuracy of description, an eye to color, a tendency to enter into details that almost wearies. It has been seen how indefinite the monster, Grendel, is in the poem of *Beowulf.* The Keltic mind could not so conceive a monster. It must have color and shape. Here is an instance : "As the King's people were afterward at the assembly they saw a couple approaching them—a woman and a man ; larger than the summit of a rock or a mountain was each member of their members ; sharper than a shaving-knife the edge of their shins ; their heels and hams in front of them ; should a sackful of apples be thrown on their heads not one of them would fall to the ground, but would stick on the

[1] W. K. Sullivan, introduction to O'Curry's *Customs and Manners of the Ancient Irish*, vol. i., p. 40.

points of the strong, bristly hair which grew out of their heads; blacker than the coal or darker than the smoke was each of their members; whiter than snow their eyes; a lock of the lower beard was carried round the back of the head, and a lock of the upper beard descended so as to cover the knees; the woman had whiskers, but the man was without whiskers."[1] These are tangible monsters; they can be drawn and painted.

With the Kelt, color is a passion; the Teuton has but the mere dawnings of susceptibility to color. Two heroes meet in battle. Ferdiad says to Cuchulaind:

"What has brought thee, O hound,
To combat with a strong champion?
Crimson-red shall flow thy blood
Over the trappings of thy steed;
Woe is thy journey!"[2]

Not of wounds or of slaughter speaks he, but of the flow of the crimson blood. In the same poem every warrior is described with all the accuracy of a modern passport. Here is an instance: "A tall, graceful champion, of noble, polished, and proud mien, stood at the head of the party. This most beautiful of the kings of the world stood among his troops with all the signs of obedience, superiority, and command. He wore a mass of fair, yellow, curling, drooping hair. He had a pleasing, ruddy countenance. He had a deep-blue, sparkling, piercing, terrific eye in his head; and a two-branching beard, yellow and curling, upon his chin. He wore a

---

[1] *The Banquet of Dun Na N-Gedh*, edited by Dr. O'Donovan, for the Irish Arch. Society, p. 21. This version dates from about the twelfth century.

[2] *Táin Bó Chuailgne*, in O'Curry's *Manners and Customs of the Ancient Irish*, vol. iii., p. 431.

crimson, deep-bordered, five-folding tunic; a gold pin in the tunic over his bosom; a brilliant white shirt, interwoven with thread of red gold next his white skin." [1] And so each leader is described with similar accuracy. No trait escapes. The color of the eye, the cut of the beard, the expression of the face, are all dwelt upon. One leader is described as " a man of hound-like, hateful face. He had light grisly hair and large yellow eyes in his head." [2] Later the English will learn the art of coloring. And when we come upon anything so distinctly fresh as this—

> "Fairer child might not be born: . . .
> Bright as ever any glass,
> *White as any lily-flower,*
> *So rose-red was his color* "— [3]

we may confidently set it down to a Keltic source.

Another characteristic trait of the Keltic mind is its power to satirize and its dread of satire. The poet is not only honored, he is feared as well. His blessing was supposed to secure against harm and bring good with it. Among the three things in the Welsh Triads that will secure a man from hunger and nakedness is "the blessing of a bard, a true descendant of song." [4] The Keltic nature has deeply implanted in it the sense of the ridiculous. It has a horror for sarcasm. It scrupulously avoids all that could induce it. For this reason it dreads a personal blemish, lest it give rise to a nickname or be occasion for satire. The Keltic bard was permitted to satirize the patron who refused him a suit-

---

[1] *Ibid.*, p. 92. The *Táin Bó Chuailgne* is the great epic of Ireland. The heroine is Spenser's Queen Mab, here called *Medhbh* or *Meave*.

[2] *Ibid.*, p. 93.

[3] *King Horn*, MS. in Bodleian Library, Oxford.

[4] *Relics of the Welsh Bards*, p. 80.

able return for his poem, or who even denied him anything he asked. And his satire was not supposed to be confined to words. The poet's curse was considered effective. It was a terror to kings and families. It caused fatalities to come upon man and beast. It brought sterility to the land, "so that neither corn, grass, nor foliage could grow."[1] And there still lingers among this people a vague feeling that harm comes from the satire or curse even of a ballad-maker. From the remotest times down to our own, says O'Curry, speaking of satire, "its power was dreaded in Erinn; and we have numerous instances on record of its having driven men out of their senses, and even to death itself."[2] Gaedhilic legends abound containing proofs of the prevalence of this idea. Here is one: The poet Neidhé wishes to banish Caier, the king and his uncle, from his throne; and as no king with a blemish can continue to rule, he resolves to bring one on him by means of satire. So he asks Caier for a present which he knows him to be pledged not to give away. "Woe and alas!" said Caier, "it is prohibited to me to give it away from me." This refusal gives Neidhé pretext for composing a satire. And the words of the satire are these:

> "Evil death and short life to Caier;
> May spears of battle slay Caier;
> The rejected of the land and the earth is Caier;
> Beneath the mounds and the rocks be Caier."

Thereupon three blisters appear upon the king's cheek. And the names of the blisters are Disgrace, Blemish, and Defect. And next morning, when washing himself in

---

[1] O'Curry, *Manners and Customs of the Ancient Irish*, vol. i., lect. iv., p. 70.
[2] *Ibid.*, lect. x., p. 217.

the fountain, he discovered the blisters; and forthwith he fled, "in order," says the story, "that no one who knew him should see his disgrace." [1] This is the spirit that gives force to, and makes effective, the savage onslaught of a Swift.[2]

IV.—KELTIC SENTIMENT.

But the master-trait of Keltic literature is the expression of sentiment. And this expression is inwoven with color, and form, and love for nature, and susceptibility to its charms, in a style and with a method that please and delight. No other nation possesses this aptitude in the same degree. It is from the Kelt that modern peoples learned all they possess of this power. It enters their literature as a foreign element. The poet does not digest it and assimilate it to his native way of thinking, for it does not altogether come home to him. When he meets with this intimate blending of nature and sentiment, he admires it for its beauty and transcribes it as a grace beyond the reach of his art. Here is a passage of this character, taken from the beautiful story of Peredur or Parcival: "And in the evening he entered a valley, and at the head of the valley he came to a hermit's cell, and the hermit welcomed him gladly, and there he spent the night. And in the morning he arose, and, when he went forth, behold a shower of snow had fallen the night before, and a hawk had killed a wild fowl in front of the cell, and the noise of the horse scared the hawk away, and a raven alighted upon the bird. And Peredur stood and compared the blackness

---

[1] *Ibid.*, p. 218. The story is taken from *Cormac's Glossary*.

[2] See *Gulliver's Travels*; also *A Modest Proposal*. In 1835 Surgeon Hamilton with others examined the Dean's skull. In his report the surgeon says: "The skull resembles in a most extraordinary manner

of the raven, and the whiteness of the snow, and the redness of the blood, to the hair of the lady that best he loved, which was blacker than jet, and to her skin, which was whiter than snow, and to the two red spots upon her cheeks, which were redder than the blood upon the snow appeared to be."[1] And we are further told that the sight held him so spellbound, the red spots had to be covered from his view in order to break the charm. All this is of the bone and marrow of Keltic sentiment. It reads the same in the rhymes of Chrestien of Troyes,[2] and in the more artistic poem of Wolfram von Eschenbach,[3] as it was told in the mountains of its Welsh home.

This sentiment, when woman becomes its object, assumes a caste of peculiar delicacy and tenderness. It has been seen that the Teuton's ideal of woman was that of an unsexed human being. Not so was she regarded by the Kelt. She loved him, and clung to him, and lived for him; and he in return loved, respected, and protected her. The beautiful Creidé is about to choose among her suitors. She does not, like Brunhild, make with them a trial of personal strength, nor does she condemn the rejected ones to death; hers is a more feminine fancy. He shall have her hand who can in song best describe her house and furniture.[4] A fair one

the skulls of the so-called Keltic aborigines of Northern Europe, which are found in the early tumuli of this people throughout Ireland."

[1] *Mabinogion, the Story of Peredur*, vol. i., p. 325, ed. Lady Guest.

[2] See the Parcival of Chrestien of Troyes, 1190, in the Appendix to Lady Guest's edition of *Mabinogion*.

[3] *Parzival*, (1200), ed. Simrock. For an account of the origin, meaning, and influence of the Arthurian epic cycle, see part ii. of this work.

[4] *Book of Lismore*, quoted in O'Curry. Even the freaks and fancies of human nature repeat themselves all the world over. In the Chinese

dies with the bloom of youth and the charm of beauty upon her. She has only been taken for a time from her grieving friends by the invisible beings who inhabit hill and lake in Erinn, to be restored to them at some future day. Edain, the Queen, is such a one. A mysterious stranger enters the hall, and plays with her husband a game of chess for whatever the winner demands. The stranger wins, and demands Edain at the end of a year. At the allotted hour he enters the guarded hall, and addresses the Queen:

"O Befinn,[1] will you come with me
To a wonderful country which is mine,
Where the people's hair is of golden hue,
And their bodies the color of virgin snow?

"There no grief or care is known;
White are their teeth, black their eyelashes;
Delight of the eye is the rank of our hosts,
With the hue of the foxglove on every cheek. . . ."

And after promising her all manner of ideal life he walks away with her unobserved by any but the King.[2] The visible world and the invisible world are both blended in the Keltic imagination. And whether we turn to the Gaedhilic or the Kymric Kelt we find each making both subservient to the tender regard he has for woman. Thus, in Welsh story we read this de-

---

novel *Ju-Kiao-Li*, or *The Two Fair Cousins*, which M. Abel-Remusat gave Europe, the heroine, Hongiu, takes a similar fancy. "She has made a vow against marrying a man of the ordinary sort; she is resolved upon having no one but a poet of distinguished talents; a person who can vie with herself in literature, both prose and poetry." (Chap. vi.)

[1] Fair woman.
[2] O'Curry's *Manners and Customs of the Ancient Irish*, lect. ix., vol. ii., p. 192.—Compare Goethe's *Lyric on the Erl-King*.

lightful passage : Arianrod lays a destiny upon her son "that he never shall have a wife of the race that now inhabits the earth." Gwyddion complains bitterly of it to Math. "Well," said Math, "we will seek, I and thou, by charms and illusions, to form a wife for him out of flowers." So they took the blossoms of the broom and the blossoms of the meadow-sweet, and produced from them a maiden, the fairest and most graceful that man ever saw. And they baptized her and gave her the name of Blodeuwedd, or Flower-Aspect.[1] This aërial play of fancy that couples the idea of a flower with that of a maiden in such literal relations, is preëminently Keltic. It is a beautiful conception.

And when Christianity shall have emancipated woman, and raised her up to a higher plane of action and responsibility, and initiated her in the art of adorning her soul with all virtues, the Keltic mind shall rise to the height of this conception as well ; and as it will help to build up chivalry in mediæval Europe, so will it contribute to strengthen the doctrine of the Church on the Immaculate Conception of the Blessed Virgin Mary. That doctrine is a mystery to human reason. St. Bernard scruples to admit it.[2] St. Thomas demonstrates its natural impossibility to his own satisfaction.[3] But this Keltic sentiment in the person of a Keltic theologian, Duns Scotus,[4] proclaims it as a glorious prerogative not to be denied to the Mother of God, and

[1] *Mabinogion, Math*, vol. iii., p. 239.
[2] *Life and Times of St. Bernard*, Abbé Ratisbonne, p. 265.
[3] *Summa*. P. 3ª. Quæst., xxvii., Art. 2.
[4] 1274-1308. "As a theologian, Scotus defended the doctrine first made a dogma in our times, but which is in complete correspondence with the spirit of Catholicism, the doctrine of the *Immaculata Conceptio B. Virginis*."—(Ueberweg, *Hist. Phil.*, vol. i., p. 454, Am. ed.)

forthwith the doctrine becomes more popular than ever and its influence more striking. And what is that influence? It shows itself in additional respect for woman, in a refinement of manners, in a purer literature, and in a more ideal art. "It contributes powerfully," says Henri Martin, "to the softening of manners, to the growth of charity, and it becomes for Christian art an almost inexhaustible source of inspiration."[1] In Christian times the restless Keltic spirit shall in its zeal for souls wander abroad, not only in England, but in France and Germany and Italy and even Iceland; bringing with "bell and book" learning and religion, and not forgetting its charming legends and its sweet music.

[1] *Histoire de la France*, t. iii., livre xx., p. 404.

CHAPTER III.

THE OLD CREED AND THE NEW.

I.—THE ENGLISH IN THEIR INSULAR HOMESTEAD.

THE English possess themselves of the most fertile regions in the island. The Britons who would still be free retire to the mountains of Wales, or cross the Channel to the forests of Brittany. What is the manner of life of the English in their new insular homestead? It is that we have already seen them practice prior to their conquest. They brought with them their old manners, and customs, and laws, and modes of thought. No sooner were they securely settled than they quarreled among themselves, plundered and murdered one another, chanted their war-songs, worshiped their gods, gambled, sold their children into slavery, and drank themselves into beasts, just as they had done in their days of piracy. The Britons are in possession of Christianity, but the Britons hate their conquerors with too deadly a hatred to attempt to save their souls. Among their greatest sins Beda mentions this, "that they never preached the faith to the Saxons or English who dwelt among them."[1] So for one hundred and fifty years after the landing upon the isle of Thanet,

[1] *Eccl. Hist.*, i., xxii.

the English remain in the darkness and superstitions of their old creeds.[1] They continue to call the days of the week after their gods; they give the names of these gods to places; they learn to erect temples in their honor. Thus Wanborough is derived from Wodnesbeorh; Thursley is Thunresleáh, from Thunor or Thor; Thunderhill is of the same derivation, it is Thunreshyl.[2] Their religion holds them with an iron grasp. It molds their nature; it is part of their inner life; its fatalism impels them to deeds of daring; its superstitions pervade their every action from rising to retiring; its gross materialized hereafter is their great hope in life and their consolation in death. Its practices are such as please their natures; it places no restraint upon their passions; it adds a consecration to deeds the most abominable; it sanctifies crimes the most horrible. It strengthens their selfishness. The gratification of their wish was to them such a power in the face of their fatalistic doctrines that they deified it, or rather it was Odin who was acting in them under the name Wisc.[3] And so we find places called accordingly; Wishanger means Wisc's or Woden's meadow; and we are told that in Devonshire all magical dealings still go under the common name of *wishtness*.[4] They had magic rimes and spells with which to cure diseases, mend broken limbs, and insure the successful issue of an undertaking. The flowers of the field were associated with their religion; caves and caverns were peopled with a mysterious order of beings; the very boundary-stones of their fields they placed under the protection of a god;

---

[1] *Ibid.*, cap. xxiii.
[2] Kemble, *Saxons in England*, vol. i., p. 344.
[3] Odin = O. N. Osk = Ger. Wunsch = Wisc = Wish.
[4] Kemble, *loc. cit.*, p. 346.

the heavens and the earth were enveloped in the mists of their religious mythology; but over all, and covering all, and giving meaning to all, was the gratification of self. Now, in such a religion were to be found only superstition and degradation. It possessed no ennobling element. It never could have led to a high order of civilization.

II.—Gregory the Great (550-604).

But a Roman, a Christian, who is in the hands of Providence to be the instrument by which European intelligence is to be molded for centuries, meets some English youths in the slave-market in Rome. He is taken with their appearance. Their well-built forms, their ruddy countenances, their golden hair, and bright blue eyes and fair white skin make him regard them rather as angels than men; and forthwith he burns with zeal to go among a people so fair to behold, and make their souls as fair, and bathe them in the light of the gospel. But his mission is of another kind. He is called to the chair of Peter, and under his wise directions others do the work he yearned so heartily to do. England is converted, and the germs of a new and a higher civilization are planted in the natures of her English sons. Let us make more than a passing mention of the father of this new civilization.

Gregory stamped his own and succeeding ages with the impress of his genius. He was alive to all the requirements of his time. His energy and activity were equal to every emergency. There was nothing too small to be overlooked; no power too strong for him to grapple with. He was a shrewd statesman, and yet a close student, fond of retirement, devoted to his books. One day we find him rebuking a Patriarch in the East;

another, settling some point of discipline in England or France; another, impressing the necessity of some important measure upon the Emperor; another, bewailing the distractions of his office, and sighing for the retirement of his younger days;[1] another, teaching the principles of the music that retains his name, in the schools he had founded for that purpose; and still another day, entering into the minutest details about his farm in Sicily. And withal, the numbers and excellence of his writings would do honor to a professional author. He prized learning at its true worth. He everywhere encouraged it, not indeed for its own sake, but as a means to attain philosophic and Scripture truth. He laid stress on the fact that those around him be well educated. In dress and speech he took care that nothing savoring of barbarism appear in any of his household from the least to the greatest.[2] "There was no one employed in the pontifical palaces," says Andrés, "who had not received a refined education, and whose sentiments, language, and instruction were not in keeping with the majesty of the pontifical throne."[3] He strove hard to diminish superstitions; he banished all astrologers from his presence.[4]

---

[1] "I can not restrain my tears," writes he to Leander of Seville, "when I transport my thoughts to that blissful haven whence they have dragged me."

[2] "Nullus pontifici famulantium, a minimo usque ad maximum, barbarum quodlibet in sermone vel habitu præferebat, sed togata, Quiritum more, seu trabeat a Latinitas suum Latium in ipso Latiali palatio singulariter obtinebat." Joan. Diaconus, *Vita Greg. Mag.*, l. ii., cap. 13.

[3] *Origine, etc., della Letteratura*, i., cap. 7.

[4] Ad hæc doctor sanctissimus ille Gregorius qui melleo prædicationis imbre totum rigavit et inebriavit Ecclesiam, *non modo mathesin jussit ab aula recedere*, sed ut traditur a majoribus, incendio dedit probatæ lectionis

Scripta Palatinus quæcumque tenebat Apollo.

GREGORY THE GREAT.

Piety and learning were the bulwarks with which he fortified himself against the desolating march of the barbarian. The Roman Empire was crumbling to ruins. The invading hosts, intoxicated with their success, were a chaos of disorder. From the wrecks of the old, Gregory built up a new power, which in its turn conquered the conquerors, taught them law and order, and raised them in the scale of civilization. The Lombards are especially fierce—fierce in their paganism,[1] not less fierce and intolerant in their Arianism.[2] Gregory treats them with firmness and prudence. He gains the confidence of Theodelinda, their queen, and seconded by her pious efforts he sees the whole nation adopt the true form of Christianity. Knowing their instinctive hatred for Rome, through the aid of his bishops he endeavors to promote among them a spirit of peace and harmony. With this view he caused the Lombard prelates, at their consecration, to swear that they would endeavor to preserve a just peace between their nation and the Ro-

---

In quibus erant præcipua, quæ cœlestium mentem, et superiorum oracula videbantur hominibus revelare. John of Salisbury—*Polycraticus*, l. ii., cap. 26. This is one of the most mischievous passages in the whole range of literature. It is the source of nearly all the misrepresentations historians have heaped upon Gregory. Forgetting that the word *mathesin* applied to astrologers as well as mathematicians, men gave out that Gregory hated mathematicians. A most likely thing to happen to the reformer of the calendar! Then, on a mere rumor—*traditur a majoribus*—this same flippant gossip states that Gregory burned the library on the Palatine Hill. But no historian believes the story now. Bayle does not think it worth refuting, for he does not regard the source as trustworthy. For a complete refutation of these and other equally silly charges made against Gregory, see Tiraboschi, *Storia della Letteratura*, t. ii., l. ii., cap. ii., p. 151, *et seq.*

[1] Greg. Mag., *Dialog.*, iii., cap. 28.
[2] "Wherever the Lombard dominion extended, illiteracy was its companion." Hallam, *Literature of Europe*, vol. i., p. 30.

mans.¹ Thus it was that through his influence upon clergy and rulers he concentrated in his hands and in the hands of his successors that spiritual power that was the guiding star of Christendom for a thousand years. In him is concentrated the organizing and governing genius of Rome.

The writings of Gregory wielded a wide and permanent influence. Still, it must be said that his genius was rather for administration than for writing books. He wrote a long and loving commentary on the book of Job, in which he takes sentence after sentence and moralizes upon each with diffuseness. This is the model after which commentators will write upon the sacred Scriptures for centuries. The method was misleading. But it were unhistorical to find fault with the great Pope for not rising to the height of the inspired poem.² At a time when every word and line of the text was literally regarded as a message from heaven to be taken to heart and applied to all affairs of life, both temporal and spiritual, such a method of Biblical criticism would have been regarded as little less than sacrilegious. Gregory was content with drawing from the teachings of the Holy Book the whole code of Christian morals, as he conceived them. With the same view, he also wrote a book of Homilies, which were popular during the middle ages. They became the manual of the clergy. Bishops exhorted their priests to make of them a careful and constant study. One of the questions put at the visitation of a diocese was whether each priest had a copy of them.³ At the be-

¹ *Liber Diurnus Rom. Pont.*, pp. 69, 71. See also Lingard's *Anglo-Saxon Antiquities.*

² See Cæsar Cantù, *Histoire Universelle*, t. vii., p. 428.

³ " Si habeat quadraginta homilias Gregorii, et eas studiose legat

ginning of his pontificate, he wrote a pastoral which was held in great esteem. Therein he laid down his ideal of a good pastor, the notes of a vocation to the priesthood, and the duties and responsibilities attached to the calling. The Emperor Maurice asked him for a copy of it. St. Anastasius, Patriarch of Antioch, translated it into Greek.[1] Soon we shall find Alfred give an Old English version of it to his English subjects. But the work of his especially popular at that day was his *Dialogues*. This book contributed materially to the conversion of the Lombards. It abounds in miracles and revelations of saints. It was suited to the credulity of the times.[2] Pope Zachary had it translated into Greek; an Arabic version of it was made in the eighth century,[3] and for five or six centuries afterward it was highly prized. Love for the marvelous was the taste of the age, and Gregory, in this respect, was not more enlightened. What he wrote he believed.[4] With the same credulity of his age, he was penetrated with the idea that the end of the world was at hand.[5] Thus it was that, though above his times in many respects, he was, in the prevalent notions of the day, a child of his age. But amid the varied occupations that go to fill up the busy life of this great saint, he still thinks of those fair English

---

atque intellegat." Reculfus, Bishop of Soissons, in his *Constitutions*, admonishes his clergy to have a copy of them. "Also, we admonish that each one of you should be careful to have a missal, lectionary, a book of the Gospels, a martyrology, an antiphonary, psalter, and a book of *Forty Homilies of St. Gregory*." Apud Maitland, *Dark Ages*, p. 27.

[1] Tiraboschi, ii., p. 155.   [2] See *Dial.*, iv., cap. 46.
[3] Fleury, *Eccl. Hist.*, l. 35.
[4] "D'ailleurs, il était si éloigné de l'intention de tromper, qu'il cite chaque fois son auteur." Cæsar Cantù, *Hist. Universelle*, t. vii., p. 428.
[5] *Epist.* xi., 67.

youths he had met in the slave-market; his heart yearns for the conversion of their island home; he has a certain number of English boys under the age of eighteen purchased and sent to Rome to be educated.[1] But his zeal outstrips their progress, and he sends Augustin with forty missionaries.

III.—AUGUSTIN AND PAULINUS.

In 597 AUGUSTIN lands on the isle of Thanet. Forty monks and some Frankish interpreters are with him. They form into line of procession; one of the brothers carries a large silver cross; another bears the image of the Redeemer; and as they wend their way toward the halls of Ethelbirht, they sing a litany and recite prayers for the eternal salvation both of themselves and of the people to whom they are come. Augustin towers head and shoulders above the rest.[2] But the King will not receive them into any house, "lest," remarks Beda, "according to an ancient superstition, if they practiced any magical arts, they might impose on him."[3] No doubt this precaution was taken at the suggestion of his priests. Ethelbirht receives them in the open air, and after they have explained their mission he gives them sustenance and permits them to preach in his kingdom. In all probability this concession was made through the influence of Queen Bertha, who was such a pious Catholic as became the granddaughter of St. Clothilde. They were tolerated; this was enough: the rest

---

[1] *Epist.* v., 10.
[2] "Beati Augustini formam et personam patriciam, staturam proceram et arduam, adeo ut a scapulis populo supereminerct." Gotselinus, *Vita S. Aug.*, cap. xlv.
[3] *Eccl. Hist.*, i., cap. 25.

soon followed. The holy, continent, self-sacrificing lives of these pious monks were more eloquent than words. Men's hearts were won. The religion inspiring such a mode of life must come from Heaven; it must be true; it must be followed. Such was their practical reasoning. The King was converted; the people went with him. Augustin's hands were full; his zeal put forth all its strength. He was naturally a timid man, scrupulously exact, most conservative of all the practices and customs in which he had been trained, careful to consult with Gregory on the smallest points of doctrine and discipline; but his saintliness and devotedness made up for whatever lack of natural parts there might have been in him. The heart of Gregory is gladdened at his great success. He sends him more laborers to reap the vast harvest—among others, Paulinus, afterward Archbishop of York. With them he sends vestments, sacred relics of the apostles and martyrs, ornaments for the churches, and many books.[1]

No doubt, among these books were the *Homilies* and *Pastoral* and *Morals* of Gregory. When Augustin first lands in England, he has with him a library of nine volumes. It is scant, but characteristic. This library is made up of the following books: 1, The Holy Bible, in two volumes; 2, the Psalter; 3, the Gospels; 4, another Psalter; 5, another copy of the Gospels; 6, the Apocryphal Lives of the Apostles; 7, the Lives of the Martyrs; 8, an Exposition of the Gospels and Epistles.[2] Of these nine volumes, six are Scriptural, and one is explanatory of the Scriptures. Thus it is that the first

---

[1] *Eccl. Hist.*, cap. 29.

[2] "Hæ sunt primitiæ librorum totius Ecclesiæ Anglicanæ," says the "Canterbury Book." Edwards, *Memoirs of Libraries*, chap. ii., p. 100.

English library is Scriptural. We shall soon find English letters saturated with Scriptural thought and colored with Scriptural allusions. And English gratitude has recorded its obligations to Augustin in these touching words: "Then it is after the number of eight days and nine, that the Lord took Augustin into the other light—happy in heart because here in Britain he had made earls obedient to him for the will of God as the wise Gregory commanded him. I have not heard that before him any other man or more illustrious bishop ever brought better lore over the briny sea. He now rests in Britain among the men of Kent in the chief city, near the celebrated minster."[1]

PAULINUS is the apostle of Northumbria. Ethelberga, the daughter of Bertha, goes to that pagan land to wed Edwin, its pagan king. Paulinus accompanies the young bride to her new home; he has but one thought in going into that benighted land: it is the thought and the hope of converting its people to the new faith. He is ever on the alert. He seizes upon any the least occasion to make it subserve this purpose. But during the first year his efforts are barren. Perhaps his too great anxiety was as much in the way of his success as the hardness of the hearts he was working upon. Still his zeal is finally rewarded. Edwin calls together his priests and chief thegns, to determine upon the feasibility of adopting the new religion. There were in that assembly some thoughtful men. One of them, a thegn, stood up and spoke an idea that must have frequently occupied his mind. It was well pondered over. It remains one of the most perfect utterances that have come down to us from that time: "The present life of man, O

---

[1] *Anglo-Saxon Calendar; Menologium, seu Calendarium Poeticum*, London, 1830, S. Fox.

King," says this thegn, "seems to me, in comparison of that time which is unknown to us, like to the swift flight of a sparrow through the hall wherein you sit at meat in winter, with your thegns and ministers, and a good fire burns on the hearth, while the storms of rain and snow prevail abroad. The sparrow flies in at one door and tarries for a moment around the light and heat of the hearth-fire, and then passes out at the other into the dark winter whence it had come. So this life of man appears for a short space, but of what went before, or what is to follow, we are utterly ignorant. If, therefore, this new doctrine contains something certain of these, let it be followed."[1] Others spoke in a similar strain. The chief priest was there, thoughtful and resolute. He was a whole-souled man, and plain-spoken, and opposed to shams and frauds under any shape or form. An honest, upright heart was his. For some time past he had been wavering in his belief in Thor and Woden. No doubt he had been a careful observer of the ways and doings of Paulinus; the holy life of the latter was an eloquent appeal to his naturally good heart. Be this as it may, Coifi, for such was his name, opened the council by a speech in which he expressed his doubts concerning the old creed, and signified his intent of placing no obstacle in the way of the new doctrine. It was a hint to the more bigoted among his fellow priests to keep in the background. They took it and remained mute. Then Paulinus explained the new creed. His very appearance was so striking that it has been left on record: "He was tall and slightly stooping; he had black hair, and a thin, pale face, and slender hooked nose, and he looked venerable."[2]

[1] Beda, *Eccl. Hist.*, lib. ii., cap. 13.
[2] Alfred's *Beda*.

There was conviction in his countenance, and his imperfect words brought conviction to his hearers. Coifi was the first to break the silence that ensued. He arose and said: "I have long since been sensible that there was nothing in that which we worshiped; because the more diligently I sought after truth in that worship, the less I found it. But now, I freely confess that such truth evidently appears in this preaching as can confer on us the gifts of life, of salvation, and of eternal happiness."[1] He counsels the King to set fire to the temples. He asks and obtains the privilege of being the first to desecrate that of Godmanham, and overthrow its idols. The labors of Paulinus were blessed beyond his most sanguine desires. This occurred in A. D. 627.

IV.—Relapse and Recovery.

But England was not yet converted. And the history of the struggle between the new creed and the old best reveals to us the character of the people. The missionaries were too few for the large harvest. People admitted to baptism by the thousand, and on the impulse of a moment, could not be well instructed. They little knew what they were doing. Their chief concern was to follow in the footsteps of their chiefs and their kings. With them they forsook their idols; with them they attended the services and the preachings of the missionaries. It was for the cunning and deceitful a new means of finding favor with their leaders; it was for the indolent an easy means of keeping themselves clear of suspicion and consequent trouble; only for the pure and simple-hearted was the new religion a revelation. The people, seeing the good monks in favor with

[1] Alfred's *Beda*.

their rulers, made it a point to show them respect. But when these same monks went outside the kingdom of their protectors they met with a far different reception. Once, when Augustin and his companions were passing through that part of England now known as Dorsetshire, they were driven away with violence, and the tails of fishes were fastened to their robes.[1] This instance might have shown Augustin the aërial structure he was erecting. It was a warning to him that to build solidly he must dig deep down; to make the new religion permanent he should seek to establish it among the people. Be this as it may, it is certain that with the passing away of the Christian rulers the country relapsed into idolatry. The three surviving bishops in the south lost all hold upon the people. Two of them fled into France; the third was on the point of following them, when a sense of duty grew upon him and overcame his fears, and he remained. The harvest of Paulinus also passed out of his hands on the death of Edwin. He fled with his ward, Queen Ethelberga, and her children to the home of her father, never to return to the land in which he had toiled with such zeal, patience, and apparent success. The English child of impulse rushed back to the religion in which he had been rooted for centuries with a rebound swift and strong as was the rush with which he had embraced the new faith.

Again the work of conversion begins. This time it comes from another source. Ireland sent her missionaries. She was then the sanctuary of learning in the West. Men and youths from England and the Conti-

[1] Gotselinus, *Vita S. Aug.*, cap. xlv.; Montalembert, *Monks of the West*, vol. iii., p. 391; *Lives of the English Saints—St. Augustine*, 241–244.

nent flocked to her schools. The venerable Beda informs us that all were willingly received, and were supplied with food, furnished books, and taught gratuitously.¹ So great was the influx of students that they were compelled to encamp in military fashion around the school.² The classic authors of Greece and Rome were read side by side with the early Fathers of the Church and the Divine Gospel.³ Greek had become such a passion that even Latin was written in Hellenic characters.⁴ We have already described this people. Its missionaries were to be found in Europe and Asia. They were men as fond of travel as they were of lore; but they were fonder of souls than of either. Among those who left their native land was COLUMKILL, a man of noble blood, but of still nobler character. He was learned; he had an insatiable thirst for books; with the instinct of a scholar, he considered no labor too great to procure a new manuscript. His was a fervent soul raised above all manner of meanness. He was a patriot, loving his native land with his last sigh. He was a poet. But he was above all a monk, attached to his monastery and loving the cell in which he enjoyed

---

¹ *Eccl. Hist.*, iii., cap. 27.

² "In the present instance we have abundant authority elsewhere to show that at and before and after the time of Adamnan (who died in the year 702), such in fact were the crowds of stranger students that flocked to some of our great schools of lay and ecclesiastical learning, that they were generally obliged to erect a village or villages of huts as near to the school as they conveniently could; and, as in Adamnan's case, to find subsistence in the contributions of the surrounding residents.". O'Curry, *Manners and Customs of the Ancient Irish*, lect. iv., vol. ii., p. 80.

³ The Berne Codex of Horace is considered by Orelli to be as early as the eighth century.

⁴ Reeves's *Adamnan*, pp. 158, 354.

the sweets of prayer and meditation, and transcribed the sacred Scriptures in his own neat hand. In 565 this pure soul built a monastery on the island of Iona. It soon became famed for its learning and piety. Numbers flocked to enroll themselves under its great founder. Other houses were established. Finally, in 635, Oswald asked and obtained some of those Irish monks to preach the Gospel in his kingdom. AIDANN was sent him. No better man could he have received. He was zealous, pious, learned, charitable, and indefatigable; especially noteworthy was his meekness. So long as he could not speak in English, Oswald acted as his interpreter.[1] Even when traveling he studied; and those who kept him company either read the Scriptures or committed psalms to memory with him.[2] In a few years Northumbria was restored to the Church. CEDD, after having successfully labored with others among the Mercians, brought the priceless boon back to the East Saxons. And so the good work went on till England became Catholic. The year of apostasy came to be regarded with such horror that it was dropped out of the records; the names of the apostate kings were erased, and no dates assigned to their reigns.[3]

V.—SHADOW AND SUBSTANCE.

Contemplate for a moment this transition from the old faith to the new. There were many points in the latter which were within the grasp of the popular intelligence, for they only expressed in a new and a purer form things already known. They were told of a hereafter; they already had faith in a future life. The

---

[1] Beda, *Eccl. Hist.*, iii., cap. 3.
[2] *Ibid.*, cap. 5.
[3] *Ibid.*, iii., cap. 9. See also the *Saxon Chronicle*, A. D. 634.

doctrine of the resurrection was explained to them; of that too they had some notions. They were told of a place of punishment; our very word for that place has come from the name of a goddess who presided over a similar one in their beliefs; Hel was the mistress of the cold and joyless world destined for cowards and traitors. They were told of a place of reward for the good and virtuous; they had themselves often dreamed of Odin's halls and the great Valhalla. They were told that there is but one God; that truth came to their minds like the recollection of a half-forgotten story; they had had some faint idea of it; there was little or no difficulty in clearing away the erroneous parts with which it was coupled. They were told of three persons in one God; that was a mystery in the presence of which they dared not reason; yet they remembered how Woden and Hænir and Lodur were the three powers that took part in the creation of man. They were told that one of the Divine Persons of the Holy Trinity came on earth as a new-born Babe, that He grew up and lived among men and was put to death—not through any guilt of His own, for He was innocence itself—but to satisfy His Father for the sins of men; that was to them a story of absorbing interest. They compared it with their myth of Baldr. They remembered how he—the beautiful, the innocent, the good and amiable Baldr, the beloved of gods and men—was killed through the malice of Loki; and in the second coming of Christ they recognized an analogy to the returning of Baldr at the end of time. The new account threw light upon, while it gave point to, the old myth. One was the shadow of which the other is substance. And when a detailed narrative of the life and death of the Divine Saviour was given them, their hearts were touched; their generous natures were moved; they were easily led to turn their indignation on themselves and do penance for those sins that were the cause of so much suffering. Then, again, the chief festivals of the Church coincided with their holidays. Christmas occurred about the same time with their midwinter Yule-tide. The Resurrection of the Redeemer was celebrated about the season that they did homage to their goddess Eostre. So far, their understandings easily glided into the new way of thinking. But when there was question of the practice of its precepts, they found themselves short of its requirements. In their bones were imbedded the vices of centuries; in their blood ran the ferociousness of the Vikings; in their minds was the lawlessness of the Bersekir. How change it all? It might not be done in a day, or in a year, or in a century. Christianity does not change human nature so suddenly. It destroys none of man's passions. It only regulates them. It teaches him how to divert them into channels of usefulness.

The old mythology had a strong hold upon English thought; it modified English expression; it originated English words. From Nicor, the spirit of water, are derived the term water-nixies and the more familiar one of "Old Nick."[1] The old mythology supplied names to their flowers. That known as "Forniotesfolme," or Forniot's hand, is so called from Forniot, the old god of the North. It gave some of our most significant words. Little think we, when saying an individual brags, that we are applying the name of a heathen god. But so it is. Bragr is one of the Œsir-gods, famed for wisdom and eloquence; and the art of poetry was called

[1] Wedgwood derives the term from Platt-D. *Nikker*, the executioner or neck-twister. (*Trans. Philol. Soc.*, vol. v., No. 105. Paper read February 21, 1851.) I prefer the derivation in the text.

"bragr." But this god is upbraided by Loki for not being more warlike and fond of battle.[1] He is regarded as a loud talker and a little doer. Here already is the idea attached to one who brags. And the names of the days of the week, as well as those of Yule-tide and Easter, are so many relics of the old creed. The same is true of the May-pole. Unconsciously, it is a perpetuation of the rites originally performed in honor of Phol.[2] So also is the tradition of the boar's head a relic of heathen superstitions. "It is not going too far," says Kemble, "to assert that the boar's head, which yet forms the ornament of our festive tables, especially at Christmas, may have been inherited from heathen days, and that the vows made upon it in the Middle Ages may have had their sanction in ancient paganisms."[3] Other superstitions also held their own in spite of the new creed. Some of them donned a Christian garment. Such was that celebrated charm for a sprained limb. In the old Continental homestead, it ran as follows:

Phol endi Wôdan	Phol and Wodan
Vuorum zi holza,	Went to the wood,
Da wart demo Balderes volon	Then of Balder's colt
Sin vuoz birenkit;	The foot was wrenched;
Thu biguolen Sinthgunt	Then Sinthgunt charmèd him
Sunnâ era suister;	And her sister Sunna;
Thu biguolen Frua,	Then Frua charmed him
Volla era suister;	And her sister Folla;
Thu biguolen Wôdan	Then Wodan charmed him

[1] Edda. Thorpe, *Northern Mythology*, vol. i., p. 28.

[2] "In England richtet man allgemein am ersten Mai einen sogenannten *May-pole* auf, wobei zwar an *pole, pfal, palus* ags. *pol* gedacht werden kann; doch dürften Pol, Phol anschlagen." Grimm, *Myth.*, p. 581.

[3] *Saxons in England*, vol. i., p. 357.

Só he wola conda:	As he well could do: [*of blood*
Sosé bénrénki, sosé bluotrenki,	*Both wrench of bone and wrench*
Sosé lidirenki;	*And wrench of limb;*
Bén zi béna,	*Bone to bone,*
Bluot zi bluoda,	*Blood to blood,*
Lid zi geliden,	*limb to limb,*
Sôse gelimida sin.[1]	*As if they were glued together.*

In the new island home this charm was given a Christian turn. It is no longer Wodan and Baldr who have power to cure; that has been transferred to the Holy Trinity, and especially to the Third Person. So the conjury was made to run thus, while a black woolen thread with nine knots was wound round the injured limb:

"The Lord rade,
And the foal slade;
He lighted,
And he righted;
Set joint to joint,
Bone to bone,
And sinew to sinew;
Heal in the Holy Ghost's name."[2]

A religion so imbedded in the popular thinking can not be easily uprooted. It is only by a long course of training that the fancy and imagination can be brought to run in the new groove of thought. To that end does the Church bring to bear all her teaching and discipline. By degrees she weeds out the tares of the old faith, and plants the seeds of the new. She finds special difficulty in getting this people to forget its hea-

[1] Kemble, *ibid.*, p. 864. This was discovered in 1842, "on the spare leaf of a MS.," at Merseburg.

[2] Chalmers's *Nursery Tales.* A similar charm exists in Holland and Belgium.

then mythology, its heathen songs, and its heathen rites, especially in connection with wakes and burials. Council after council issues decree after decree; but at first with slight success. A more effectual method was at hand. A great genius was about to sing the glories of heaven and earth and make Christian truth so acceptable in song that the popular mind willingly lets the heathen imagery drop out of its memory and in the stead fills it with Scripture thought and Scripture allusion. Who that genius was and what his influence was we shall now inquire.

CHAPTER IV.

WHITBY.

I.—St. Hilda.

AND first a word upon her who fostered the genius of Cedmon.[1] Rest we on the sea-beaten cliffs of Whitby. It was then known as Streanshalh, and received its more

---

[1] Mr. Palgrave (*Archæologia*, vol. xxiv., p. 342) weaves this theory about the poet's name: "Now, to the name Cædmon, whether considered as a simple or as a compound, no plain and definite meaning can be assigned, if the interpretation be sought in the Anglo-Saxon language; while that very name *is* the initial word of the book of Genesis in the Chaldee paraphrase, or Targum of Onkelos: *b'Cadmin* or *b'Cadmon* (the *b'* is merely a prefix) being a literal translation of *b'Raschith* or 'In principio,' the initial word of the original Hebrew text. It is hardly necessary to observe that the books of the Bible are denominated by the Jews from their initial words: they quote and call Genesis by the name of b'Raschith; the Chaldaic Genesis would be quoted and called by the name of *b'Cadmin*, and this custom, adopted by them at least as early as the time of St. Jerome, has continued in use until the present day." The word Cædmon is not found in the Old English dictionaries; but the word *Ced* is, and means boat, or wherry; so that Cedmon would mean boatman or wherryman. It is a name still common in Yorkshire. Writing in the last century, Lionel Charlton says: "Cedmon's memory remained in great veneration, not only at Streanshalh, but also through the whole kingdom of Northumberland, where his name was long honorably used as an appellative or proper name, and after the Conquest was adopted as a surname; so that there yet remain to these our days some families in Whitby and its neighborhood that are known by the name of Cedmon or Sedman; a name with us the most honorable and ancient of all others." (*History of Whitby*,

modern name only from the Danes. The zealous and devoted Bishop Aidann is still actively at work. It was in 640, at Hartlepool, that he founded the first nunnery in Northumberland, and placed at its head an Irish lady named Heru. Later on he builds a monastery at Whitby. He appoints to govern it the Abbess HILDA. A most remarkable woman was this saint. Baptized at the age of fourteen by Paulinus, she preserved unspotted the robe of innocence with which, on that day, she was clothed. She lived with her relatives and friends till the age of thirty-three, when she entered a convent in East Anglia and consecrated herself to God. Thence she is called by Aidann to govern the new-built monastery at Whitby. It is a double monastery, having a house for men and one for women, according to a custom prevalent in those days.[1] With both is Hilda

b. i., p. 17: York, 1779.) Bouterwek, an authority of great weight on such subjects, finds no difficulty in deriving the name from an Old English origin. In a learned dissertation on the subject he says: "Ipsum Cedmonis nomen (cf. Gr. Gr. 2, 507) initio appellativum fuisse, dubium non est. Variæ ejus formæ sunt: Cedmon, Cædmon, Ceadmon, vox ipsa composita e *mon*, vir (cf. Paraphr. p. 89, 3: flotmon nauta, p. 186, 12; vraec-mon, fugitivis), et *ced*, quod ut in glossis a Cl. Monio editis est (p. 331) lintrem denotat. Cedmon tamen non nautam signifiĉare videtur, sed potius idem valere quod *scegdhmon*, pirata, a *scegdh*, *sceidgh* liburna, scapha (cf. Gr. 3, 437, ibique Gl. Monii). Hoc vero nomen nihil infame habuisse, alia ejusmodi veterum nomina, e. g. *landsceatha* latro, hros-dioph, heriwolf, beowulf cet. satis luculenter testanter (cf Gr. Gr. 3, 785, notam). (*De Cedmone, Elberfeldæ*, p. 9.) Such stress need scarcely be laid upon the mere name were it not for some attempts to build up a theory, to which Mr. Henry Morley inclines, that the Irish monks received their teachings and traditions, not from Rome, but from the East. This is a theory for which the writer, after a diligent search, has been able to discover no foundation.

[1] See Lingard's *Antiquities of the Anglo-Saxon Church* for examples and authorities, pp. 82, 83; also *Vit. St. Liobæ* apud Mabillon, Sæc. 3.

charged, and well and efficiently does she govern them. The monastery of men becomes a shrine of learning and science, and is noted as the nursery whence issued several saintly bishops. The prudence, tact, and holy life of the abbess extend their beneficial influence far beyond the convent-walls. Bishops and kings consult her under difficulties.[1] Contesting parties refer their feuds to her and abide by her decision. Her tact in this respect was noteworthy. No one ever thought of appealing from her word. She died in 680, in her sixty-third year, deplored by all, and left in the north of England a name undimmed by centuries. Her memory is still kept green by the gratitude of a people to whose ancestors she was a benefactor. Everything strange or wonderful in the neighborhood of Whitby occurs through her interposition. Nothing hurtful might approach her abode. Wild geese could not fly over her monastery.[2] Ammonites abound in that district; to the fancies of the people they are snakes turned to stone by the dear St. Hilda. Under favorable circumstances a mirage may be seen in one of the windows of the ruins of the church still standing; it is the dear St. Hilda, who continues to show her love for the good people of Whitby, by watching over them from this window.[3] Childish fancies these of a childlike people,

---

[1] Butler, *Lives of the Saints*, vol. iv., p. 370.

[2] Camden.

[3] A paper that was formerly printed and sold in Whitby alludes to these legends. It may be found in Grose's *Antiquities of England*, vol. vi., p. 163. Therein St. Hilda is represented as speaking in the following rude verses, written with more affection than good taste:

> "Likewise a window there I placed,
> That you might see me as undressed:
> In morning gown and night-rail there,
> All the day long fairly appear.

who thus embody their gratitude and devotion in legend which outlives history and hard fact. By us she is to be remembered as the person who encouraged and drew out the genius that was to revolutionize the popular heathen mind. She was the fast friend of Cedmon.

II.—The Story of Cedmon's Life unraveled.

The life of Cedmon lies buried in fable and obscurity. But through the mists in which his name is enveloped we can discern enough whereby to know that he was advanced in years before he became a monk; that prior thereto he was an eminently pious man; that he sought rather to obey the dictates of his conscience than to please men; that his genius was appreciated in his own day, and that he was regarded as one of the brightest glories of his age. The first glimpse we get of him is at festivals and entertainments. On such occasions, when the guests were well filled with meat and warmed up with beer, it was customary for each to contribute to the common amusement of all by singing a song. To this we find Cedmon uniformly objecting. When he saw the musical instrument approach, he arose from the table and went home. At first sight such conduct would mark him as being unsocial. Why might he not let the harp pass him by? Others there were who could not sing, and still who remained and enjoyed the occasion. The usual penalty for such delinquencies was to be compelled to take a certain quantity of beer in one drink. He might have paid the penalty or allowed himself to

> At the west end of the church you'll see
> Nine paces there, in each degree;
> But if one foot you stir aside,
> My comely presence is denied;
> Now this is true what I have said,
> So unto death my due I've paid."

be mulcted in some other way, and not have persistently marred the pleasures of the festival by leaving in so abrupt a manner. Reason there must have been, and reason there was, for the strange proceeding. Cedmon's was no sullen disposition. It is not, as the Venerable Beda informs us, because he could not, so much as because he would not sing, that he left the festive hall so frequently. His companions knew that he could sing, and in all probability anticipated from him the crowning effort of the occasion. It was to avoid their displeasure and perhaps their anger by a direct refusal, that he chose to leave at some favorable moment prior to the placing of the harp in his hand. And what were those songs he did not choose to sing? They were not the pretty sentimentalities of modern drawing-rooms. Such things were unknown in Cedmon's day. They were not soundings of the deeper feeling of love. That too, as has been seen, was unknown to the English nature as a sentiment to be sung and played with. "That cultivated feeling," says Sharon Turner, "which we call love, in its intellectual tenderness and finer sympathies, was neither predominant nor probably known. The stern and active passions were the rulers of society, and all the amusements were gross or severe."[1] They might have been martial lays; but to these Cedmon would scarcely have objected. He who sang so well of the warrings of the angels in heaven, and described so graphically the submersion of Pharaoh's hosts, could not find it in him to refuse to chant a strophe of the Fight of Finnesburgh, or sing the deeds of Beowulf. He had sung them from boyhood; he had been fired by their spirit; he knew them by heart; they were part of his thinking. Not to these did he have repugnance; but there

[1] *Anglo-Saxons*, vol. iii., p. 263.

was another species of song popular at festivals, which it grieved his soul to listen to. It was the mythic deeds of Thor and Odin, and the other pagan gods, that he refused to sing. "It might easily be proved," says Dr. Guest, "that our fathers had poems on almost all the subjects which were once thought peculiar to the Edda."[1] And there was still another kind of poetry, which was at first connected with the rites and ceremonies of the pagan religion, and which, long after these rites and ceremonies had fallen into disuse, continued to be sung at festivals and wakes. It was a practice common to many of the Teuton races. And the songs used were generally of a most unspeakable character.[2] Now, as late as the middle of the ninth century, Leo IV. forbade the Saxons to sing the diabolical hymns which the common people were accustomed to sing over their dead.[3] This was the singing that shocked Cedmon's Christian sensitiveness. It clouded the sunshine of his naturally convivial disposition. He felt that it was unworthy of a Christian's lips to utter, or a Christian's ear to listen to. He saw that no good came of it. And once he was at an entertainment in the neighborhood of Whitby Abbey; the company was in a rejoicing mood; the beer flowed freely; the harp was taken up; one of the feasters began to sing; the song was of this objectionable kind. Cedmon could not endure it; he left the hall in sadness. With heavy heart he went out to the stable to take care of the horses. It was the custom for one of the company to guard the horses during the night; for at this

---

[1] *English Rhythms*, vol. ii., p. 241.

[2] Thus of the Lombards did Gregory the Great write: "More suo immolaverunt caput capræ diabolo, hoc ei per circuitum currentes et carmine nefando dedicantes." *Greg. M. Dialog.*, iii., cap. 28.

[3] See Wackernagel, *Das Wessebrunner Gebot*, p. 25.

time honesty was not one of the English virtues, and
theft was considered a crime only when detected. In
his solitude the heinousness of these pagan songs among
a Christian people weighs him down. It is a thought
that has been growing upon him. For some time past
he has been asking himself if there is no way by which
to banish this last remnant of paganism still clinging to
the English mind. While revolving the subject in his
heart, he looks across the plain and discerns the lights
from Streanshalh stream in upon him. He remembers
the Abbess Hilda; he thinks of the good monks who
live under her mild and motherly protection; he is not
unmindful of the calm and peaceful life they lead; he
contrasts it with the rude scenes through which he has
frequently to pass. He remembers the boisterous feast-
making from which he came, and then he thinks that
just at that very moment those good monks and nuns
are also rejoicing, but after another fashion. They too
express their sentiments in canticles of gladness and
sorrow as varied as the emotions of human nature.
"There," he said to himself, "is heaven upon earth;
there are men and women leading angels' lives, and, like
those around the throne of God, singing the praises of
their Creator." Thereupon he muses upon heaven; he
remembers the angelic choirs; he feels his soul within
him flutter with eager desire to sing of the abode of the
blessed, of the creation of the world, of the ways of
Providence toward men; and then and there he deter-
mines to render himself worthy of the honor of singing
of these high themes by purifying his heart still more,
and making it a fitting instrument to be played upon by
the Divine Hand. He resolves to consecrate the remainder of his days to the noble purpose of making poems
that will supersede the shameful songs that still bind so

many Christian hearts to the pagan world of thought. Then and there does he feel the new mantle of inspiration descend upon him; he sings the creation; he dreams of it; he remembers the next morning the lines he had composed the night previous; he also remembers his good resolution. He goes to the "town-reeve, who is his caldorman,"[1] and tells him of his purpose. The latter brings him to the Abbess Hilda. He repeats to her the introductory lines he improvised on the Creator and His works. She calls together several of the learned men in her monastery, and has Cedmon to repeat his verses before them; for she is first desirous of knowing whether the verses he repeats are his own, or whether or not he is an impostor. But they all of them are favorably impressed with his rare talents. "They concluded," says Beda, "that heavenly grace had been conferred on him by our Lord." Still they resolve to put him to a further test. They recite for him some passages from the Holy Scriptures; these they explain to him, and request him to compose some verses on them. He goes home, constructs his poem, and returns next morning with the whole idea done up in most excellent poetry. St. Hilda is delighted. Embracing the grace of God in the man, she encouraged him to adopt the monastic habit.[2] He did so, and she associated him with the brethren in her monastery, leaving instructions that he be taught sacred history. And as he learned its meaning and spirit, he turned various parts of the sacred Scripture into English poetry.

The English language had never before clothed such

[1] Alfred's translation of Beda.
[2] "Unde mox abbatissa amplexata gratium Dei in viro, sæcularum illum habitum relinquere, et monachicum suscipere propositum docuit." *Hist. Eccl.*, lib. iv., cap. 24.

sublime thoughts. Never was its power of expression stretched to its full bent. None but the greatest genius could render it adequate to the themes. But Cedmon was equal to the task. He succeeded admirably. His poems became popular. "The revolution," says Guest, "effected by Cedmon appears to be complete."[1] All imitation of his works only showed how inimitable they were. "Others after him," says Beda, "attempted, in the English nation, to compose religious poems, but none could ever compare with him."[2] He created that intense and earnest religious feeling in the popular mind which was so prevalent down to the days of the Venerable Beda.[3] The pagan hymns became less frequent. The strong light of his bright song dimmed their last rays. Expressions so forcible and verses so harmonious laid strong hold upon the popular thinking. The man singing so beautifully must have been inspired by Heaven. So thought the people. And some among them had a dim recollection of a great poet who had been first a shepherd, and, having learned how to sing in a dream, remembered what he had composed in his sleep, sang it next day and continued to sing beautiful things till death. It mattered little to them about the name; but among them was a poet who must have learned after some such manner. Let us recall the earlier myth. It is related of Hallbiörn that he was a shepherd lad who watched his flock near by the grave of the poet Thorleifr. One day he took it in his head to sing a hymn of praise in honor of the poet; "but," we are told, "because the lad was entirely uneducated, he was unable

[1] *Rhythms*, ii., p. 241.
[2] *Ecclesiastical History*, b. iv., ch. 24.
[3] Wright, *Essay on Anglo-Saxon Literature*, in *Biographia Britannica Literaria*, vol. i.

to carry out his pious design. Then, one night did the hillock open up, and a stately man walked up to the shepherd, touched his tongue, repeated a verse aloud for him, and returned to his grave. When Hallbiörn awoke he remembered the verse which he had heard, and from that day forth became a celebrated poet." [1] Thus it was that Cedmon had come to be regarded as a divinely inspired shepherd.

III.—The Themes Cedmon sang.

Once more we catch a glimpse of the man. He himself lifts the veil for us. He is at the pinnacle of his fame; old age is closing upon him with an iron grasp; friends are dropping away from him into the grave; the old faces have passed; the new ones may have more admiration for his genius, but he can not make them bosom friends. A large stone cross is to be erected. It is a costly monument, a great artistic effort for that day. Our Lord is represented as standing on two swine. A Latin inscription tells us that He is a judge of equity, and that the wild beasts acknowledge the Saviour of the world in the desert.[2] Lower still Paul and Anthony are pictured breaking their loaf in the desert; another Latin inscription speaks the fact. But, as in olden times similar stone monuments had the praises of some heathen god inscribed in Runic characters, so is it now desired

---

[1] Bouterwek, *Cædmon's Dichtungen*, *Vorrede*. Cf. Grimm, *Myth.*, 855. Pausanias relates a similar tradition of Æschylus: "Æschylus says of himself that when a boy he once fell asleep in a field, where he was watching some grapes, and that Bacchus appeared to him in a dream and exhorted him to write tragedies." (Lib. i., cap. xxi., 2, p. 28, ed. Dindorfii.) Pausanias lived about A. D. 170.

[2] "Jesus Christus judex æquitatis. Bestiæ et dracones cognoverunt in deserto salvatorem mundi."

to have a Christian hymn perpetuated upon this. Who is so capable as Cedmon ? Time and again, as he himself tells us, has he composed such inscriptions. And into this, his last, he seems to have thrown his whole soul. He has a dream, in which the Rood speaks to him and recounts its feelings and emotions as the Redeemer was transfixed to it:

"Methought I saw a Tree in mid-air hang—
Of trees the brightest—mantling o'er with light-streaks;
A beacon stood it, glittering with gold."[1]

Long lay he, looking with sorrow upon the Healer's Tree—*Hœlendes treow*—till at last it spake and told how it grew upon the wood's edge, was cut down and set upon a hill. It says :

"I spied the Frey[2] of man with eager haste
Approach to mount me; neither bend nor break
I durst, for so it was decreed above,
Though earth about me shook."

And then the Rood tells the whole story of the suffering and death and burial and resurrection of the Saviour. It further speaks of its becoming honored since that memorable event, though once it was reckoned "hardest punishment, loathliest among men, ere life's way it had made straight and broad to speech-bearing mortals." For which it considers itself honored more than all other trees, even as—

[1] " Thuhte me thæt ic gesawe syllicre treow
·On lyfte lædan, leóhté bewunden,
Beama beohrtost. Eall that beacen waes
Begoten mid golde."

[2] Frey is the god of peace. When its mythological significancy was lost, it became an epithet of honor for princes, and is found frequently applied to our Lord and God the Father. Notice that Cedmon

> "His Mother, Mary's self, Almighty God
> Most worthily hath raised above all women."

And now the poet enters into himself and expresses his great confidence in obtaining salvation through the Cross. This confidence is all the greater inasmuch as he hath sung its glories so frequently:

> "Soul-longings many in my day I've had,
> My life's hope now is that the Tree of Triumph
> Must seek I. Than all others oftener
> Did I alone extol its glories;
> Thereto my will is bent, and when I need
> A claim for shelter, to the Rood I'll go.
>   Of mightiest friends, from me are many now
> Unclasped, and far away from our world's joys;
> They sought the Lord of Hosts, and now in heaven,
> With the High-Father, live in glee and glory;
> And for the day most longingly I wait,
> When the Saviour's Rood that here I contemplate
> From this frail life shall take me into bliss—
> The bliss of Heaven's wards: the Lord's folk there
> Is seated at the feast; there's joy unending;
> And He shall set me there in glory,
> And with the saints their pleasures I shall share."[1]

gives the expression to the Rood, but nowhere in the poem uses it himself.

[1] *The Ruthwell Cross.* The Runic form of this poem was first correctly deciphered by Kemble. The whole poem was afterward found in the Vercelli Book. The dialect of the lines on the Ruthwell Cross is regarded by Mr. Kemble as "that of Northumbria in the seventh, eighth, and even the ninth centuries" (*Archæologia*, vol. xxviii.). Professor George Stephens made a special study of the Cross and discovered an additional Rune attributing the poem to Cædmon. It reads: *Cædmon mæ fauætho*. See *The Ruthwell Cross*, by Professor George Stephens, F. S. A., London, 1866. The version in the Vercelli Book is in more modern dialect than that in Runes.

The poem breathes throughout charity, sweetness, piety. It is a dream, an allegory, the forerunner of the numerous dreams that subsequently figure in English literature : of Langland's, and Chaucer's, and Lydgate's, and Dunbar's, and John Bunyan's. But this wail of Cedmon for the friends of other days, with which the poem closes ; this longing hope soon to join them ; this living by anticipation in the celestial mansions—is the last glimpse we get of the man till the hour when his desires are to be fulfilled and his poetic soul passes from the beauties of earth to the bliss of heaven.

Living in so elevated a sphere of thought, Cedmon could find it in himself to write nothing but what tended to elevate and spiritualize the aspirations and emotions of human nature. The Venerable Beda bears testimony to this effect : "He never could compose frivolous and useless poems, but those alone pertaining to religion became his religious tongue."[1] But withal, wide was the range of his themes. He did not confine himself to the mere paraphrasing of Scripture, or allegorizing upon the Rood. He also sang of the Divine attributes ; of the judgments and the mercy of God to men ; of the beauty of virtue and the hideousness of vice ; but he sang with such fervor and persuasion that he led many from their evil ways to the practice of good deeds. This is no fictional assertion. The historian takes the pains to inform us of it. "By his verses," says the Venerable Beda, "many were often excited to despise the world, and to aspire to heaven." As they became part of the people's thinking, the recollections of paganism faded out into the dim mists of

[1] "Nihil unquam frivoli et supervacui poematis facere potuit ; sed ea tantummodo quæ ad religionem pertinent, religiosam ejus linguam decebant." *Hist. Eccl.*, lib. iv., cap. xxiv.

the past, occasionally to be remembered in order to weave a legend about some Christian great one, such as that they applied to Cedmon himself.

IV.—The Secret of Cedmon's Success.

The secret of his success was twofold—it lay in his great genius and in his holy life. Of the first it is not easy at this distance of time to form an adequate idea. Conceive a people with the ignorance and mental inaction of centuries weighing them down and making them of the earth, earthy; knowing only the use of the instruments of war and the chase; brutal in their habits; material in their thoughts; their uncouth natures slightly glossed with a varnish of Christianity; Christian indeed in name and in creed, but pagan in many of their customs and manners—conceive all this, and then remember that this people is daily witnessing scenes of war and bloodshed. The old English chroniclers record them with an admirable coolness: "A. 658. This year Kenwalh fought against the Welsh at Peonna. . . . A. 661. This year, during Easter, Kenwalh fought at Pontesbury, and Wulfhere, the son of Penda, laid the country waste as far as Ashdown. . . . And Wulfhere, the son of Penda, laid waste Wight, and gave the people of Wight to Ethelwalde, King of the South Saxons, because Wulfhere had been his sponsor at baptism. . . . A. 675. This year Wulfhere, the son of Penda, and Escwin, the son of Cenfus, fought at Beaden-head. . . . A. 676. And Ethelred, King of the Mercians, laid waste Kent. . . . A. 679. This year Elfwin was slain near the Trent, where Egfrid and Ethelred fought, and St. Etheldrida died." The death of a saint, a battle, the slaying of a man, are all told in the same breath; they are all of them events of almost daily occurrence.

THE SECRET OF CEDMON'S SUCCESS. 111

These are the scenes in which Cedmon lived and moved. In the midst of all this din he raised his voice and was heard. He sang the substance of which all the ancient myths were but the shadow. He led men to forget more and more the pagan past ; to exchange the dirges on the death of Baldr for the doleful strains on the Saviour's passion ; to let the glories of Valhalla become dimmed by the more spiritual and real splendors of the heavenly kingdom. This was a great work ; it was a noble task ; it was molding the popular mind into new shape ; it was helping to spiritualize their natures ; it was preparing the soil for the seeds of grace. None but the greatest genius could have achieved it all. He brought the Oriental imagery of the Bible within the comprehension of the humblest English mind ; he draped it in the English fashion of thinking ; he made its purely spiritual language palpable to the English imagination. He did it in language musical and flowing. His verses have been the admiration of all those who gave them attention. "His accent," says Guest, "always falls in the right place, and the emphatic syllable is ever supported by a strong one. His rhythm changes with the thought—now marching slowly with a stately theme, and now running off with all the joyousness of triumph, when his subject teems with gladness and exultation."[1]

But the holiness of his life no less than the strength of his genius added weight to his words, and made them strike with such force. The Venerable Beda bears testimony to his virtues. He was an eminently religious man, fond of prayer, devoted to the reception of the sacraments of the Church, attentive and punctual in the performance of his various duties. He was

[1] *Rhythms*, ii., p. 50.

a cheerful worker in God's service, submissive in all things to the will of his superiors, happy when he saw others the same; but he was the terror of those whom he found disorderly and lagging in their duties toward their Creator. Having entered religion late in life, he was prepared to appreciate its quiet, peaceful, undisturbed ways, as he contrasted them with the fickleness and boisterousness of the world he had abandoned, and he thought that others should in this respect feel as he felt. His happy, cheerful disposition—always prepared with a kind word or a pleasant saying—tended to make the religious life attractive to others. There was nothing gloomy in his piety. He was no friend of moroseness. This last he regarded in its true light, rather as a hindrance than a help to genuine religious feeling. Leading such a life, how else could his death be than happy also? And such the Venerable Beda tells us it was. Let us linger over his last days, and watch the going out of that brilliant meteor of English song. To be able to stand by the death-bed of England's first great poet is a rare privilege. For some time a disease, the nature of which is not mentioned, had been undermining his constitution; during two weeks he felt it weakening him beyond recovery; and now he feels that the day of his dissolution is at hand. Nothing daunted, he moves about among his brethren; his cheery soul sheds sunshine into their hearts; in whatever mood he finds them, he leaves them with a laughing face and a pleasant thought. The evening of this last day he walks over to the infirmary, and asks those in attendance to prepare a bed for him, which they do with no small share of surprise. He stays up till after midnight, keeping everybody enlivened with his pleasant conversation. Midnight passed, he asked to communicate in the reception of the holy Eucharist. And they answered: "What need of the Eucharist? for you are not likely to die, since you talk so merrily with us, as if you were in perfect health." But he insisted on receiving it, and according to the custom of that day it was placed in his hands. He then asked those around him whether they were all in charity with him and free from rancor. There was only one answer—a unanimous "Yes." How else could they be with such a genial companion, holy religious, and great poet? He was full of life and humor; he had frequently made them laugh, but it was not at the expense of charity, it was not by giving pain to others. So, when the same question was put to him immediately after, well might he say, "I am in charity, my children, with all the servants of God." But the ruling passion asserted itself even in death. Cedmon desires to hear once more the praises of God sung, before he goes to sing them in heaven in union with the angelic choirs and the friends who passed before him. He would have his soul wafted upon the song of prayer and benediction ascending from the chapel near by. So he asks how soon the time was when the brothers were to sing the nocturnal praises of the Lord; and, when told that it was not far off, he said, "Let us await that hour"; and, signing himself with the sign of the cross, he laid his head on the pillow, and, falling into a slumber, his soul passed away.[1] A death befitting his life.

Let us now address ourselves to that which still lives of him—his spirit as embodied in his poetry.

[1] Beda, *loc. cit.*

V.—CEDMON AT WORK.

Cedmon's genius, in its first flight, disdains all midway courses, and soars into the celestial empyrean. With the deeds of human heroes he is familiar; but he will none of them. In praise of his holy Creator alone—Heaven's Ward—will he attune his harp. The gods of his English ancestors have been extolled; right proper is it then that the true God—the Glory-King of hosts—have a lay dedicated to Him. And so the poet bursts forth into a most eloquent prelude; every word is brimful of meaning; every line bends beneath the weight of his theme, and word and line show each alike how he labored to grapple with his subject in a manner adequate to its dignity:

> "Mickle right it is that we, heaven's guard,
> Glory-King of hosts! with words should praise,
> With hearts should love. He is of powers the efficacy;
> Head of all high creations;
> Lord Almighty! In Him beginning never
> Or origin hath been; but He is aye supreme
> Over heaven-thrones, with high majesty
> Righteous and mighty."[1]

Never, in the history of Old English thought, was such a poetic beginning heard. It is the song of a soul strong in its convictions of the greatness and majesty of Him it extols. This is the passage said to have been composed by the poet that memorable night he watched in the stable. Then follows a brief account of the rebellion and fall of the angels, which, in all probability, was the theme given him by the learned men of the community as a test; for he afterward reverts at length

---

[1] Guest's translation in *English Rhythms*, vol. ii.

to the same subject. The description is vividly English. God is a stern Overlord who treats his adversaries with an iron hand. "Stern of mood he was; he gript them in his wrath; with hostile hands he gript them, and crushed them in his grasp." This was succeeded by peace. On earth, it was a rare thing in his day; so he sings of it in heaven:

> "Then as before was peace in heaven—
> Fair peaceful ways; the Lord beloved of all—
> The ruler of His Thanes—in splendor grew;
> The good all bliss full-sharing with their Lord." [1]

As the subject grows upon the poet in all its greatness, he also rises with it. Could we be witnesses of the labor with which, as he pondered over verse after verse of the Bible, he struck out those flashes of light that shone in his day, and are not yet dimmed, we would see a giant-like struggle between matter and spirit; the limited utterance and the unbounded desire; the strong determination breaking up the new field of poesy with fierce energy. He read the opening of Genesis. The awful sublimity of those words penetrated him: "And the earth was void and empty, and darkness was upon the face of the deep, and the Spirit of God moved over the waters." [2] Some expressions in it reminded him of his old English cosmogony. "The earth was void and empty": "This," thought he, "is the Ginunga-gap, the yawning abyss, of which my an-

---

[1] "Tha waes sóth swa ær, sibb on heofnum—
faegre freotho-theawas; frea eallum leof—
theoden his thegnum—thrymmas weoxon;
dugutha mid drihtne dreám-hæbbendra."
                    Thorpe's *Cædmon*, p. 5.

[2] Genesis i. 2.

cestors sang. I must sing of it too without introducing the flesh and bones of Ymir." Therefore he sang:

"Here yet did naught exist save cavern shade,
But deep and dim did stand this wide abyss."[1]

And in these lines, if the poet remembered, he also anticipated. The "wide abyss"—*wída grund*—is the Ginunga-gap—the yawning abyss—of the Edda; but so also is the "cavern shade"—*heolster-sceado*—the "darkness visible" of Milton.[2] Again, the coloring of the older poems of his English ancestors clings to his description of things in that beginning of times. He remembers how it was sung: "When Ymir lived no earth was found, nor heaven above; one chaos all, *and nowhere grass*."[3] These were not the words, but they were clearly the idea in his mind when he dictated or penned these lines:

"Earth's surface was
With grass not yet begreened; while far and wide,
The dusky ways, with black, unending night,
Did ocean cover."[4]

Thus he worked in the smithy of his brain, as he hammered out his golden verses. Thus he brought the Scripture-thoughts within the grasp of the popular mind. But as he advances he leaves behind him still more the imagery of the past, and accommodates himself more closely to the new order of ideas. Even his meter

---

[1] "Ne waes hér thå giet nymthe heolster-sceado
wiht geworden, ac thes wída grund stôd deôp and dim." *Ibid.*
[2] Cf. Job x. 22.   [3] Edda.
[4] "Folde waes thå gyt
graes ungréne: gårsecg theahte
sweart synnihte side and wido,
thonne waêgås." *ll.* 122–'5.

changes to suit his mood. Thus, when discoursing on heaven and on the prerogatives of Satan, the line lengthens out into most solemn expression:

> "So fair was he made—so beauteous his form
> Received from the Lord of hosts—he was bright
> As are the bright stars. His task was to praise
> The works of his Lord; his heavenly joys
> To cherish most dear; their Giver to thank
> For beauty and light upon him bestowed."

Long might Satan have enjoyed his glory in heaven. But he began to plot. The poet read of it in Isaiah: "How art thou fallen from heaven, O Lucifer, who didst rise in the morning? how art thou fallen to the earth, that didst wound the nations? And thou saidst in thy heart: I will ascend into heaven; I will exalt my throne above the stars of God; I will sit in the mountain of the covenant, in the sides of the north; I will ascend above the height of the clouds; I will be like the most high."[1] Upon this passage he builds up a long argument of plotting on the part of Lucifer:

> "'Wherefore,' he said, 'shall I toil?
> No need have I of master. I can work
> With my own hands great marvels, and have power
> To build a throne more worthy of a God,
> Higher in heaven. Why shall I, for His smile,
> Serve Him, bend to Him thus in vassalage?
> I may be God as He.
> Stand by me, strong supporters, firm in strife.
> Hard-mooded heroes, famous warriors,
> Have chosen me for chief; one may take thought
> With such for counsel, and with such secure
> Large following. My friends in earnest they,

[1] Isaiah xiv. 12-14.

> Faithful in all the shaping of their minds;
> I am the master, and may rule this realm.'"[1]

Such rebellious language is severely punished. Satan and his adherents are cast into the infernal regions. These the poet also describes at length. Here again he combines the Scripture account of hell with the ancient English idea of it. To his ancestors fire had no terrors; it was rather the cold, dreary, inactive life that made hell unendurable to them. Therefore, Cedmon combines the two ideas:

> "Each fiend through long and dreary evening,
> Hath fire renewed about him; cometh then,
> Ere dawn, an eastern wind, fierce cold upon it—
> The dart of fire or frost must rankle there—
> Some hard affliction each must ever have."[2]

In this abode of suffering Satan addresses his companions in misery. He bemoans his plight. He surveys the torments by which he is surrounded. But the most unendurable of all is the thought that Adam is to take his place in heaven. Here the poet has some truly sublime touches. He combines, in a rare degree of excellence, dramatic action with descriptive power. The abrupt manner, and the sudden turn of expression, couched in the strongest language possible, speak of an enraged soul. We miss fiendish acuteness, but we find in its stead pride and churlishness enough:

---

[1] Morley's version in *A First Sketch of English Literature*, p. 19.
[2] "Thaer hæbbath heo on éfyn ungemet lange
 ealra feonda gehwilc, fyr édneowe:
 thonne cymth on uhtan easterne wind,
 forst fyrnum cald symble fyr oththe gàr
 sum heard geswinc habban sceoldon."

"And Satan spake—he who in hell should rule,
Govern th' abyss henceforth—in sorrow spake.
God's angel erst, in heaven white he shone,
Till urged his mind, and most of all his pride,
To do no honor to the Lord's sweet word.
Within him boiled his thoughts about his heart;
Without, the wrathful fire pressed hot upon him—
He said: 'This narrow place is most unlike
That other we once knew in heaven high,
And which my Lord gave me; though own it now
We must not, but to Him must cede our realm.
Yet right He hath not done to strike us down
To hell's abyss—of heaven's realm bereft—
Which with mankind to people He hath planned.
Pain sorest this, that Adam, wrought of earth,
On my strong throne shall sit, enjoying bliss,
While we endure these pangs—hell-torments dire—
Woe! woe is me! could I but use my hands
And might I be from here a little time—
One winter's space—then with this host would I—
But press me hard these iron bands—this coil
Of chain—and powerless I am, so fast
I'm bound. Above is fire; below is fire;
A loathlier landscape never have I seen;
Nor smolders aye the fire, but hot throughout.
In chains; my pathway barred; my feet tied down;
Those hell-doors bolted all; I may not move
From out these limb-bands; binds me iron hard—
Hot-forged great grindles! God has griped me tight
About the neck.'"

And so Satan continues addressing his associates, asking them to stand by him and not fail in the strife. "Heroes stern of mood—renowned warriors—they have chosen me for chief." The whole passage reminds one of the sublimest strains in *Paradise Lost*. There is less reasoning in Cedmon; he is more objective; the sufferings of his Satan are all physical, except the one pang of envy he feels at the thought that man is to be installed in his place. Milton is more subjective; his Satan despises the mere physical pain; it is the agony of mind incident upon humiliation and defeat that weighs upon him. Cedmon tells us of his hero's pride; we feel the pride of Milton's Satan. This difference is due to the respective ages in which they lived. In Cedmon's day men did not analyze feelings and emotions; they acted and suffered and endured and spoke out the results of their thinking rather than its processes. When Milton wrote, thought was more developed; men were more reflective and analyzing, and it was natural for them to enter into the springs and motives of action.

But man must be made to share these hell-torments. So forthwith Satan undertakes to tempt him. He arrives in the garden of Paradise. There are the trees of good and evil. "The fruit was not alike. . . . The one was so pleasant, so fair and beautiful, so soft and delicate." He might have life eternal who ate of that. "There was the other, utterly black; that was death's tree, which much of bitter bare." There was no mistaking them. Satan pretends to be a messenger from God. Adam receives him with suspicion; tells him he understands God's commands, but naught of what he says. Satan pretends displeasure, threatens his Master's vengeance for the insult offered. Thereupon Adam asks him for some pledge or token by which he may know him to be sincere; but Satan has none, and forthwith, like a good keeper of his Overlord's place, Adam bids him begone: "Therefore I can not thee obey, but thou mayst take thee hence." But Satan, nothing daunted, "turned him wroth of mood to where on earth's realm he saw the woman Eve standing, beautifully formed."

With her he is successful in his evil design; for the poet takes care to assure us, "to her a weaker mind had the Creator assigned."[1] But Cedmon treats Mother Eve with great tenderness. He seeks to palliate the evil she brought upon herself and the whole human race: "Yet did she it through faithful mind; she knew not that hence so many ills, sinful woes, must follow to mankind." However, the deed is consummated, and now it is Satan's turn to rejoice: "Then laughed and played the bitter-purposed messenger." Such is the story of the Fall, as sung by Cedmon. He sings it as he might have sung any domestic episode. We would not take it as the measure of his power. But later on, when he describes the flight of the Israelites and the destruction of Pharaoh, the poet is at home. Then the whole strength of his genius breaks out. The old Bersekir blood rises in him. He is no longer the historian, nor is he the translator. He is the true poet, the seer. The vision is before him in all its dread reality. The old spirit that used to be fired with such themes as the Battle of Finnesburgh, inspires him to rival that soul-stirring poem. We will not attempt a metrical version. We prefer transcribing a literal rendering; it retains more of the original fire. See, for instance, with what an apparent relish he paints preparations for battle: "They prepared their arms; the war advanced; bucklers glittered, trumpets blared, standards rattled; they trod the nation's frontier; around them screamed the fowls of war; the ravens sang greedy of battle—dewy-feathered. Over the bodies of the host—dark choosers of the slain —the wolves sang their horrid even-song." This is the language of one who has vividly before him what he

[1] "Hæfde hire wacran hige
Metod gemearcod." *Cædmon,* Thorpe's ed., p. 87.

pictures to the mind's eye. And now the destruction of Pharaoh and his host begins. Note the torrent of words in which it is told:

"The folk were affrighted, the flood-dread seized on their sad souls; ocean wailed with death; the mountain-heights were with blood besteamed, the sea foamed gore; crying was in the waves, the water full of weapons; a death-mist rose; the Egyptians were turned back; trembling they fled, they felt fear; gladly would that host find their homes; their vaunt grew sadder; against them, as a cloud, rose the fell rolling of the waves; there came not any of that host to home, but from behind inclosed them fate with the wave. Where ways ere lay sea now raged. Their might was merged, the streams stood, the storm rose high to heaven, the loudest army-cry the hostile uttered; the air above was thickened with dying voices; blood pervaded the flood, the shield-walls were riven; shook the firmament that greatest of sea-deaths. . . . The bursting ocean whooped a bloody storm the seaman's way; till that the true God through Moses's hand enlarged its force, widely drove it, it swept death in its embrace. . . . Ocean raged, drew itself up on high, the storms rose, the corpses rolled. . . . The Guardian of the flood struck the unsheltering wave of the foamy gulfs with an ancient falchion, that in the swoon of death these armies slept."[1]

Here is destruction with a vengeance. It was with full zest the poet undertook to recount it: "The bursting ocean whooped a bloody storm . . . . the storms rose, the corpses rolled." Were we not told that it was all the work of the true God, we might well imagine we had found another relic of the Vikings in their fierce pagan days. It is in such passages, in which we pass behind the poem and its Scriptural basis, that we are enabled to measure the strength of the poet's genius. He

[1] *Cædmon*, xlvii., p. 206, Thorpe's edition.

not only speaks the old language ; he also thinks in the old routine of thinking, with his thoughts somewhat purified ; but there is no ideal above that of personal bravery or brute force ; anything higher was yet beyond the grasp of the Old English mind ; the spiritual element is there, but it is still a foreign element. The poet never rises above the sublimities of the Bible ; he frequently lowers them to bring them within the compass of the popular thinking. His heaven is no longer the Valhalla of the Teutonic North. It becomes a costly, well-ordered church : " There the gate is golden, fretted with gems, with joys encircled for those who into the light of glory—to God's kingdom—may go ; and round the walls appear beauteous angel-spirits and blessed souls—those who from hence depart ; where martyrs give delight to the Creator and praise the Supreme Father—the King in his city—with holy voices." Had he spoken otherwise he would have been ill understood ; his genius would have failed of reaching the general intelligence. He would not have fulfilled his mission.

VI.—CEDMON'S INFLUENCE AT HOME AND ABROAD.

The poetry of Cedmon was a revelation to the people. It brought the sublime thoughts of the Bible within their grasp. It enlarged their views of Christian teachings. It solved in a manner primitive enough, but satisfactory for them, some of the questionings that must have arisen in their souls on hearing recounted the history of God's wonders from the beginning. It gave palpable shape and form to many of the mysteries of religion. The rebellion of the angels ; the fall of man ; original sin, and its consequences, became henceforth no longer vague notions, but rather, living, present things to their minds. Is it not told how the angels fought and fell, and how they were punished? Is not their abode of torment described? And have we not the very words of Lucifer? And do we not listen to Adam and Eve discoursing over the apple? Are not the words that Satan spoke to Eve recorded therein? It is all a new mythology, substituted for the old. It is a framing in which to group the truths of Christianity and the history of God's providences. Later, the same framing will be slightly modified for a similar purpose, and it will be known as the Miracle-play. Milton will adopt it in his epic, and the popular mind will be educated to regard almost as positive truths the imaginary descriptions there given of things unseen.

Cedmon educated the tastes of the people to an appreciation of the sacred Scriptures. From his day forth the Old and New Testaments become popular with the English. Henceforth they are, in a sense, the people's horn-books. And Cedmon's song is remembered and his name revered for centuries after his voice has become silent in the grave. The unknown Christian poet, who gives us the extant version of the poem of Beowulf, becomes so unmindful of the pagan people of whom he sings, that he introduces the Gleeman singing Cedmon's song of the creation:

"And sound of harp was there; sweet sang the poet;
He told the origin of men from far—
Told that the Almighty wrought the earth—the plain
In beauty bright embraced by waters;
And, victor-proved, the sun and moon did set—
Light-giving flames to dwellers on the land;
And decked earth's varied parts with boughs and leaves;
And eke created life of every kind."[1]

[1] *Beowulf*, i., 180, *et seq.*

Thus it is that the poet preserves the tradition of his brother-poet's song. And the historian, in the person of the Venerable Beda, crystallizes in his immortal pages the glory and the greatness of his name, the loveliness and saintliness of his life. Nor is this all.

In the ninth century his poems became known in France. Louis the Pious introduced them. This good monarch, not content that the knowledge of the divine books be confined to the learned and erudite, resolved, and by the interposition of Providence it was so managed, that all his subjects speaking the German language should become familiar with them. So speaks the Latin Preface to the paraphrase.[1] And, in order to show how Providence aided the King, it adds: A certain person ordered a man of the Saxon race, who was esteemed a great poet, to devote himself to the poetical translation into the German of the Old and the New Testament, so that the sacred reading of the divine precepts be opened to learned and ignorant alike.[2] There was no need for a new translation. The language of Cedmon was that of Louis. There might have been—as no doubt there were—variations of dialect; but the people of one nation understood those of the other. Long previously had commercial relations been established between them. They were Franks whom St. Augustin took with him as interpreters, on his first going to England.[3] No doubt the Preface

[1] This Preface is found among Hincmar's letters: *Magna Bibliotheca Veterum Patrum*, Labigne, Paris, 1654, t. xvi., p. 609.

[2] "Precepit namque quidam viro de gente Saxonum, qui apud suos non ignobilis vates habebatur, ut vetus ac novum Testamentum in Germanicam linguam poetice transferre studeret, quatenus non solum literatis, verum etiam illiteratis, sacra divinorum præceptorum lectio panderetur." *Ibid.*

[3] Butler, *Lives of the Saints*, ii. p. 278. And F. Schlegel, speaking

wished to pay a compliment to Louis, when it gave him the credit of ordering the translation. Be this as it may, it adds the more important information that the poet sang from the creation of the world to the end of the Old and the New Testament, interpreting and explaining as he went along so lucidly and elegantly that he delighted all who heard and understood. It then refers to his having received his powers in a dream. "It is said that this same poet, while yet entirely ignorant of his art, was admonished in a dream to arrange the precepts of the sacred law in a style suitable to his own tongue." This is evidently a tradition of the legend told by the Venerable Beda in the previous century. A poem attached to the Preface speaks still more clearly of his peasant origin.[1] That the poet was appreciated, may be learned from the rather fulsome praise of the Preface: "So great was the fluency of his works, so great shone the excellence of the matter, that his poetry surpassed all German poems by its polish. The diction is clear; clearer still is the sense."[2] And this, be it remembered, was no publisher's advertisement. It was written after the poems had been

of the poems collected by Charlemagne, makes this important remark: "I have little hesitation in saying that I believe those poems to have been composed in the old Saxon language, the same in which Alfred wrote, and which was spoken by Charlemagne himself, whenever he did not make use of Latin; for we must remember that the favorite residence of Charlemagne was in the Rhenish Netherlands, the old patrimony of the Franks, whose language was originally the same with that of the Saxons." *History of Literature*, lect. vii., p. 173.

[1] " Incipe divinas recitare ex ordine leges,
Transferre in propriam clarissima dogmata linguam;
Nec mora, post tanti fuerat miracula dicti:
Qui prius Agricola, mox et fuit ille Poeta."
Versus de Poeta, et interprete hujus Codicis. Bib. Patr., loc cit.   [2] *Ibid.*

some time among the people. It only records a fact. They had already won popular favor. And, after all, it is scarcely less praise than that bestowed on them by Beda. True, the poet is not named in the Preface; but the coincidence in the lives of the poets, in the subject-matters of their poetry, in the unanimous testimony to its excellence and influence, is too great not to admit of identity. Both are of the people; both are admonished in a dream to sing the sacred truths of religion; both sing of the creation; both paraphrase the Old and New Testaments; the productions of both are universally lauded. It is because both are one, and that one is Cedmon.

And now, it would seem as though his spirit continued to live and labor through the whole Teutonic race. In France and Germany, as well as in England, Scripture paraphrasings became the popular rage. They are the drama and the novel of the people. They are more. They are not read or listened to for amusement's sake. They are pored over and dwelt upon with passionate earnestness, to be lived and acted out. Through them, the people become familiarized with the thoughts and deeds of the Redeemer, and learn to follow them more closely. Some of these old horn-books of that day have come down to us. We have the poem called *Krist*;[1] we have a song of the Samaritan Woman;[2] we have a poem on the Last Judgment;[3] translations of several psalms, and a harmony of the four Gospels, called *Heliand*.[4] This last was widely known and highly prized. There are extant traditions of its popularity in

[1] Ottfried, Königsberg, 1831.   [2] Schilter, *Thesaurus*, vol. ii.
[3] *Ibid.*
[4] J. Andreas Schmeller, Stuttgart, 1830. This is mainly a print of the Cotton MS. in the British Museum.

Germany and England.[1] It is written in a dialect to be understood by both nations. There has been much conjecture as to the authorship. Schmeller thinks it was written by an English missionary. Grein wished to identify it with that of the translation made in the time of Louis the Pious, but with no success. Evidently this version is of the ninth century, and the production of some ecclesiastic intimate with the Scriptures, and at least aware of the apocryphal Gospels; for he tells us that many disciples of Christ endeavored to write God's holy word with their own hands in a magnificent book; only four were chosen, and to them were given "God's power, help from heaven, the Holy Spirit, and strength from Christ: *maht godes· helpa fan himila· helagna gast· craft fan christæ*." Now, be it remembered that about the time this form of poetry became so general, English missionaries returned to Christianize their kinsfolk in the old homestead; hosts of them, under Willibrord and Boniface, invaded Friesland and Germany, bringing with them the light and life of the Gospel and the Church. They were not unmindful of the experience and traditions of other days in their own country; that which was so skillful a weapon in the hands of Cedmon, and Aldhelm, and Beda himself, they did not neglect. It may have been the same songs they repeated; it was certainly the same in sense, and in the same spirit, that they sang. It is Cedmon who still speaks.

Nor is he forgotten later. The sole manuscript of his works that is known to be extant is of the tenth

[1] "Poema istud non solum in Anglia, sed etiam in Germania et quidem Wirceburgi extare, teste G. Eccardo (in *Monum. vet. Quaternione*, Lipsiæ, MDCCXX., fol. 42, et in *Comm. de rebus Franciæ or.* MDCCXXIV., tom. ii., fol. 325), jam pridem inter antiquitatum curiosos rumor fuerat."—Schmeller, *Præfatio Editoris*, p. viii.

century, and even that is fragmentary. It is divided into two books, and of these only the first is continuous; the second is hopelessly broken up. The MS. is in the Bodleian Library. It is illuminated. Some of the scenes represented are evidently those which, in that early day, must have been enacted in the Miracle-plays. The tradition of the creation and fall, as preserved in these plays, is that handed down by Cedmon. But in this manuscript we must not look for the identical poem that Cedmon sang. In passing from generation to generation for three centuries, various changes must have imperceptibly entered into the text. A version in the West-Saxon dialect might not conform to that in the Northumbrian; meddlesome scribes might occasionally undertake to improve the poem; others, again, might be too ignorant to write it correctly; and so, from one cause to another, while the general tenor would remain, special passages might read differently. This accounts for the discrepancies in the reading of the opening lines of the poem, as found in King Alfred's translation of the Venerable Beda's "Ecclesiastical History," and in the manuscript. No doubt Cedmon would be at some trouble to identify the songs he sang with the present transcript of them. But he is not alone in this respect. Imagine Tasso coming among the gondoliers of Venice as they chant his "Jerusalem Delivered." And would not Shakespeare and Æschylus be equally at a loss to recognize in our modern texts of their masterpieces the verses they indited? The MS. belonged to Usher, who gave it to Francis Junius or Dujon. This latter it was that assigned the poem to Cedmon, and as Cedmon's had it printed in 1655. And Dujon had a friend to whom he communicated his literary projects; that friend was then in his forty-seventh year, and was meditating a grand epic; he saw this MS.; no doubt he received a copy of the printed poem from his friend; it decided his subject and its treatment; the materials he had collected for a Miracle-play he made use of in this new project, and forthwith he produced a work of great genius. That man was Milton, the poem was "Paradise Lost."[1]

Here terminates the direct and immediate influence of Cedmon. Beyond whatever of expression and allusion may have been preserved by Milton, or passed into our thinking through current forms of expression, that influence is for us dead. We may rehabilitate the poet's life and imagine the times in which it was spent; but those times are past, and with them the magnetism of his influence. It remains but as a record.

[1] Johnson's "Life of Milton," *Works*, vol. ii., p. 33

CHAPTER V.

CANTERBURY.

I.—THEODORE AND ALDHELM.

PASS we from the north to the south. Leaving Whitby, let us go to Canterbury. It is the primatial see of England. It is occupied at this time by THEODORE OF TARSUS (602–690). He comes to England in his mature years. He brings with him the traditions of the East and the Greek learning. He has a copy of Homer and other classic authors, and into their beauties he initiates the youths who sit at his feet.[1] His scholars become as versed in Greek and Latin as in their mother-speech.[2] He gave an impetus to Greek studies that continued long after his death. Students wrote their prayers in the Greek language before they had mastered its alphabet.[3] He is no less skilled in the art of healing the body than in that of curing souls. He

---

[1] Lombarde says that he was shown by Archbishop Parker "*The Psalter of David* and sundry homilies in Greek—Homer also and some other Greek authors, beautifully written on thick paper with the name of this Theodore prefixed in the front, to whose library he reasonably thought (being thereto led by show of great antiquity) that they some time belonged." (*Perambulation of Kent*, 1576, p. 233; Edward, *Memoirs of Libraries*, vol. i., ch. ii., p. 101).

[2] Beda, *Hist. Eccl.*, lib. iv., cap 2.

[3] There is a MS. in the British Museum, bearing date of 703, with Greek prayers written in English characters. (MSS. Cott. Galba., A. 18.)

initiates his disciples into the secrets of medicine. And with him is a congenial soul, well versed in all the knowledge of the day; that soul is ADRIAN. He labors with his friend and superior and shares his renown. Beda speaks of him as a man most active and most prudent.[1] But Theodore has imbibed in a special manner Gregory's spirit of administration. He organizes the English Church and welds it all the more firmly with Rome. He prepares a code of public penance for sins committed, that enters into details as minute as the laws of the land. He builds churches in better style than was previously known in England. He has lead put upon the roofing, and glass placed in the windows—"such glass," remarks Eddius, "as permitted the sun to shine within."[2] In this manner does the *Chronicle* speak of his death: "A. D. 690. This year Archbishop Theodore died; he was bishop twenty-two years, and he was buried at Canterbury; and Berthwald succeeded to the bishopric. Before this the bishops had been Romans, but from this time they were English." This little comment tells more than a volume of the efficiency of the work done. English youths had been trained to the extent of being found worthy of the highest church dignities in the land. The spirit of unity and harmony was abroad.

And there were other boons brought to England by Theodore. He imparted to English youths the traditions of the East concerning the Saviour and His dis-

---

[1] "Viro æque strenuissimo ac prudentissimo Adriano." (*Vita Ben-Bis*, p. 715, Migne edition.)

[2] See Dean Hook's *Lives of the Archbishops of Canterbury*, vol. i., p. 157. This book has some merits, but its treatment of Theodore is very flippant. It does him evident injustice in attributing to him unorthodox opinions on the sacrament of penance.

ciples. He taught them the unwritten law of that mysterious land. And he encouraged them to transcribe it in their own language, and after their own fashion. Among his disciples none was more promising than ALDHELM (656–719).

MAILDULPH, "a Scot, as they say, by nation, a philosopher by erudition, and a monk by profession,"[1] settled in the place now called after him Malmesbury. He was poor in this world's goods ; but in their stead he possessed learning and zeal in abundance. Among his first disciples was Aldhelm. The reputation of the school at Canterbury under the management of Adrian attracted the young Englishman thither ; and, after perfecting himself in all the learning taught there, he returned to the poor abode of his first master, obtained a grant of the land on which it stood, applied his ample patrimony to the building of a monastery, and devoted his noble life to the saving of souls. He soon became abbot, and was afterward made bishop. He was the bosom friend and counselor of Ini and his pious queen. He was a man of varied accomplishments : a linguist knowing Latin and Hebrew, and so versed in Greek that Faricius tells us he wrote and pronounced Greek like the Greek nation ; a musician as well ; and William of Malmesbury says he had so fully imbibed the liberal arts that he was wonderful in each of them and unrivaled in all. But Aldhelm was above all a poet. He delighted in scattering figures and studied phrases over everything he said. He frequently degenerates to turgidity in his Latin works. This in a great measure is a fault of his age. Men regarded learning with a certain awe. They rejoiced in overcoming difficulties ; they

[1] William of Malmesbury, *History of the Kings of England*, b. i., ch. ii., p. 28.

looked not to results; they were content with the new thought, the new form of expression, as is the child with the new bauble. Therefore it is that Aldhelm's standard of excellence consists in making fantastic arrangements of speech and overcoming verbal technicalities. He has all the figures of rhetoric on his fingers' ends. He writes a treatise on the subject. He has a technical name for every word he pens and every expression he uses. He is a master-mechanic in the art of constructing sentences. And he knows it. Here is his sign-board: "The leaky bark of our feeble ingenuity, shaken by the whirlwind of a dire tempest, may attain late its port of silence by laborious rowing of the arms; yet we trust that the sails of our yards, swelling with the blasts of every wind, will, notwithstanding their broken cables, navigate happily between the Scyllas of solecism and the gulf of barbarism, dreading the rocky collisions of vain-glory and the incautious whirlpool of self-love."[1] This style was admired, and Aldhelm was regarded as the most accomplished writer of his day. His poetic style is more subdued. And though he invents for himself all manner of difficulties, he is still over florid. However, matter makes up for manner. Aldhelm is the knight of virginity. It is the theme nearest his heart. He writes on it in prose; he sings its praises in verse:

"See how the lilies deck the fruitful furrow;
And blusheth on its thorny bush the rose,
Which crowns the victor-wrestler and becomes
The garland for the winner in the course:
So purity, subduing rebel nature,
Wins the fair diadem which Christ awards."[2]

[1] Apud Turner, *History of England*, vol. iii., p. 405.
[2] Lib. ix., *De Laude Virginum*.

This is strange language for a descendant of the worshipers of Frigga. Could his ancestors rise in their graves they would stand agape with wonder. And still this poem was not merely understood in Aldhelm's day; it was admired; the reading of it led a queen to embrace the state he extolled so eloquently.[1]

But this elegant scholar is not content with writing Latin poems for learned nuns.[2] He also ministers to the wants of the people. His heart beats in sympathy with them; he yearns to see them elevated into a more refined and more spiritual atmosphere; he knows the power of poetry over their slow-moving intelligences; he applies the gift with which he has been endowed, and sings for them in their mother-speech. Forgetting his learning, he brings himself down to the level of those children in intellect, and makes use of language and expression within their grasp. Forgetting his dignity, he stands on a bridge and sings for them hymns so sweet and impressive that two centuries later—in the days of Alfred—they still linger in the popular memory. What these hymns were we may best learn from the specimens that have come down to us from the school of Theodore and Adrian. One of them has been attributed to Aldhelm by Jacob Grimm. That it belongs to his age is certain; that it was written by him is probable.[3]

[1] Cuthburga. William of Malmesbury, *History of the Kings of England*, § 35.

[2] See Lingard's *Anglo-Saxon Antiquities*, ch. x., p. 189.

[3] It is also highly probable that the original MSS. of his English poems were destroyed when the Malmesbury Library was sacked and its valuable contents scattered. "An antiquary who traveled through that town many years after the dissolution, relates that he saw broken windows patched up with remnants of the most valuable MSS. on vellum, and that the bakers had not even then consumed the stores they had accumulated, in heating their ovens." (Apud Maitland, *Dark Ages*, p. 281.)

II.—The Poem of Andreas.

That poem is called *Andreas*.[1] It is a legend of St. Andrew and St. Matthew. The pious curiosity of the first Christians naturally asked what became of the apostles, and their imaginations soon filled in the details history failed to give. They became the themes of a new epic cycle.

Each apostle traveled into distant lands, and worked miracles, and converted the people, and became a hero in the land of which he was an apostle. It was a new conquest of the world. And so it had its poets. An episode of this cycle is *Andreas*.[2] St. Matthew, with his disciples, is taken prisoner by a cannibal people called

---

[1] Text: It is found in the MS. discovered by Blume in Vercelli, in 1836. Jacob Grimm published it with notes and introduction in 1840. In 1853, J. M. Kemble edited it for the Ælfric Society. Kemble is disposed to place the poem in the eleventh century. But though his scholarship is unquestionable, he is so very arbitrary in his speculations that his remarks have to be taken with caution. I am disposed to adopt Grimm's views for these reasons:

1. The poem is based upon a Greek MS. called Πράξεις 'Ανδρέου καὶ Ματθαίου, and after the eighth century the study of Greek died out in England. This Greek MS. may be seen in the *Bibliothèque Nationale* at Paris.

2. The old epic form of expression is too predominant for any period later than the eighth century.

3. When the poet becomes personal, he speaks of his own style in the same depreciatory manner we have already seen Aldhelm use. He tells us that he has spoiled the song beyond his power, and that a more learned than he must sing the rest.

4. It is evident that the original legend must have been introduced by Theodore or Adrian. Their disciples learned it, and who more apt than Aldhelm? Who more ready to put it in verse?

[2] "The *Codex Apocryphus Novi Testamenti*, published by Fabricius, contains a brief abstract of this legend." (T. Arnold, *Manual of English Literature*, 4th ed., p. 12.)

Mermedonians. St. Andrew is warned by a voice from heaven to go to his aid. At first he raises objections; but being reassured that all would be well, he resolves upon setting out:

> "Then was the errand to the noble champion
> Proclaimed in the town: not slack was his intent,
> But steadfast, hard, and noble-minded he
> In his great work; no skulker from the battle;
> Ready for war; to do God's battle stout,
> And bold in thought, he went at break of day
> Across the sand-hills to the seashore,
> His thegns with him—upon the sand they went.
> The ocean sounded, loud the sea-streams dashed;
> He hopeful grew when on the strand he found
> A ship wide-bosomed. Came resplendent morn,
> Of beacons brightest hastening o'er the waves;
> From out the darkness heaven's candle shone
> Holy o'er the lake-floods." [1]

The peaceful Andrew is made a war-beast, a chief with his following. It is the old epic casing in which is put the simple thought that he prepared and went down to the seashore. A boat is in readiness manned by no less personages than the Deity and two of his angels. "Near the sea-warder, then sat himself the holy one—noble by the noble. Never heard I that in a comelier ship laden with lofty treasures men sat, glorious kings, beauteous thegns." [2] This is a reminiscence of the saga of Woden playing the ferryman to deliver men from danger. A storm arises; ocean roars; the abyss is excited, deeply vexed. It is proposed that the followers of Andrew go to the land and await his return. But like true thegns they prefer to share his dangers. "We shall be odious

[1] *Codex Vercellensis*, ed. Kemble, p. 15.
[2] *Ibid.*, p. 21.

in every land—hateful to the people."[1] This we have seen to be one of the first principles instilled into the English youth. Andrew and his companions fall asleep, and in the morning find themselves lying on the beach in Mermedonia. Unseen he enters the city: "The man famous of mood stepped on the street; the road directed him; none of men might recognize—none of the sinful see—him; the Lord of triumphs had upon the plain fenced the dear chieftain with his protection."[2] Here is the work of the mythical tarn-cap without the name. Thus protected he comes to the prison. The seven guards drop dead: "Death destroyed them all; powerless they fell; the death-rush clutched them, a sword-bloody hero."[3] Easily might we imagine that it is another Grendel who is playing havoc. The traditional epic style clings throughout to the descriptions. Andrew's touch opens the prison-door. Hear how the poet tells it: "Soon he attacked the door through hand-touch of the Holy Ghost, and entered there, mindful of valor, the man a war-beast." The Christian narrative and the heathen wording are distinctively visible. Andrew enters. Matthew is rejoiced to see his bosom-friend: "Each clasped the other in his arms; they kissed and embraced each other." Matthew and his companions are released, and, like the Israelites of old, pass out of the town under a pillar of cloud. We are told their number. It was two and a hundred and forty and women besides. Here ends the first part of the story.

And now comes the hour of trial for Andrew. The people expect to feast on the prisoners. Rage seizes them

---

[1] *Codex Vercellensis*, p. 23.   [2] *Ibid.*, p. 57.
[3] "Ealle swylt fornam,
Druron dômleáse, deathrœs forfeng,
Hæleth heorodreorig" (*ll.* 1988-'91).

when they realize their disappointment. But they must have human food. So they cast lots among themselves. The lot falls upon an old man; but he gives them his son in his stead. Andreas pities the youth, and prays to God for him. Him God defended "holy from above against the heathen people; he commanded the weapons of the men, likest unto wax, in the onset to melt away."[1] So in *Beowulf*, the good sword of the hero had no effect upon the monster. A demon reveals Andrew to the people. In their rage they seize and drag him among the "mountain dens and along the streets paved with stones of many colors." Wounded and exhausted, he is thrown into prison, and then a cold winter's spell sets in. Here is the poet's description: "Snow-bound the earth with winter-casts, cold grew the storms with hard hail-showers; and rime and frost, hoary warriors, locked up the dwellings of men. . . . Frozen were the lands; with cold icicles shrunk the water's might; over the river-streams the ice made a bridge, a pale water-road." Here is more than personation. "Rime and frost, hoary warriors": these were real gods in the Northern mythology.[2] But Andrew suffers not; his wounds are healed before morning, as were the wounds of the heroes of old in the Northern sagas; and from the blood he lost sprung up blooming bowers. "Then looked behind him the dear champion; . . . he saw blowing bowers stand, laden with blossoms, where before his

---

[1] J. Grimm, *Andreas und Elene*, p. 34.
[2] "*Frost* the old Norse seer discerns to be a monstrous, hoary Jötun, the giant *Thrym* or *Hrym*. . . . *Rime* was not then, as now, a dead chemical thing, but a living Jötun or devil; the monstrous Jötun *Rime*, drove home his horses at night, sat 'combing their manes'—which horses were *Hail-clouds* or fleet *Frost-winds*." (Carlyle, *Heroes and Hero-Worship*.)

blood had spilled." His virtues and his miracles finally triumph. The Mermedonians are converted; they now hold him in honor and veneration. But Andrew, after confirming them in the faith, and appointing a bishop over them, departs to his own country.

Here ends the story as told in this old poem. The diction is pure, the descriptions are labored; the poet evidently looks to his style. He even calls our attention to it; or rather, he calls the attention of the two whose good pleasure he especially consulted in writing the poem: "Yet shall ye two, in little bits, further recite a portion of my sayings."[1] The two here referred to are, in the opinion of Jacob Grimm, Ini, King of Wessex, and his Queen Ethelburga, of whom Aldhelm was the friend and counselor.[2]

III.—CYNEWULF.

Another poet of the same school, whose works have come down to us, is CYNEWULF. "He was," says Grimm, "a contemporary, probably a pupil, of Aldhelm's."[3] After the example of his master in his Latin poems, he distributes the letters of his name throughout his English poems in Runic characters. We know nothing of him except what little he reveals to us in his works. From that little we infer that in his youth he

[1] "Hwæthre git sceolon
Lytlum sticcum leoth worda dael
Furthur reccan." (l. 1487.)

[2] Kemble here objects that the word *git*, ye two, is not the dual form. He translates the expression thus: "Yet will I still, in little fragments, words of song relate." But Mr. T. Arnold, whose knowledge of Old English is unquestionable, thus renders it: "Yet must ye two, in little pieces, further con over a portion of my verses." (*Man. Eng. Lit.*, p. 14.)

[3] "Cynewulf war wohl ein zeitgenoss, vielleicht ein schüler Aldhelms." (*Andreas und Elene, Vorrede*, 21.)

had been wild : "I was stained with my deeds, bound in my sins";[1] that misfortunes of one kind or other came upon him : " Buffeted with sorrows, . . . with misery compassed"; that entering into himself he changed his manner of life, studied for the priesthood, and was ordained : " Till He laid knowledge on me through the bright ordination, for a comfort to me in my age ; a blameless grace the powerful King measured out to me "; that then it was his mind was opened and he learned the strength of his intellect and exercised it in the congenial labor of singing of Christ and His saints and His Holy Cross.

1. He sang the story of the finding of the Holy Cross by St. Helena. This poem is called *Elene*.[2] The poet takes care to tell us that he had well digested the subject as he found it in books before putting it in English song : " Not once alone, but often, had I the tree of glory in remembrance ere I about the bright tree had revealed the miracle, as I found in books in the courses of events announced in writings concerning the tree of victory.[3] The book from which the story is taken is a *Life of Cyriacus*[4] and it copies even its historical inaccuracies with close fidelity. Constantine is about fighting a battle. The night previous to the engagement he has a dream in which he sees the holy Rood. He consults his wisest men upon the meaning of his dream. A Christian among them explains to him the mystery of the cross. He has it inscribed on a banner.

[1] *Elene*, Codex Vercellensis, canto xv.

[2] Text: 1. Grimm, in the same volume with the *Andreas*. 2. Kemble, in his edition of the *Codex Vercellensis*. 3. Grein's *Angelsächsische Poesie*, b. ii.

[3] *Ibid.*, canto xv.

[4] See *Acta Sanctorum*, May 5th, and Kemble's Introduction to the Vercelli Book.

It strikes terror in the enemy, though tenfold the number of Constantine's army. The victory leads to Constantine's conversion, and he receives baptism at once. This part of the poem is the most spirited. The description of the battle is such as pleased the English taste. But it differs in no essential from the battle-scenes in the older epic cycles. The same traditional accompaniments are found : "The troop of people went, a war-song sang the wolf in the wood. He shrank not from the rune of slaughter; the eagle, dewy-feathered, raised his song upon the track of the foe.[1] The rest may be found in substance in Cedmon's Paraphrase. Constantine then commands his mother to proceed to Judea with a troop of warriors to find where is hidden the true Cross. Here the poet gives more of the old traditional descriptions. Men and arms and the sea are all painted as we found them in *Beowulf.* The one new element in the picture—Helena—is thus touched upon : "Never heard I before or since that on the ocean-stream—upon the sea-street—a lady led a fairer power."[2] She arrives in Judea, and, calling the people together, she upbraids them for their cruelty to the Messiah, and sends them away to choose the wisest among them to give her the information she requires. At first they choose a thousand wise men ; then from among these five hundred are selected. After much obstinacy they give her Judas to answer her questions; but it takes seven days' fasting to break his spirit. So, going with the Queen to Calvary, he prays in Hebrew that the place of the true Cross be revealed, and forthwith smoke ascends from the spot. The Cross is recovered ; afterward the nails, out of which is made a bit for

---

[1] Grimm, *Elene.* p, 27.
[2] *Ibid.*

the horse of Constantine, which bit acts as a wonderful charm. Such, in a few words, is the story of *Elene.* It is far inferior to *Andreas* in expression and plot. But few subjects were more popular in that day. We have seen Cedmon sing the glories of the Holy Rood. Aldhelm identifies Christians with the Cross. He calls them *crucicolæ,* or venerators of the Cross.

2. Cynewulf sang the story of the martyrdom of St. Juliana.[1] A pagan youth named Heliseus loved Juliana; her father betrothed her to the man of wealth. He knew not how she loathed the youth in her mind. "To her was awe of God greater than all the treasures that in that noble's possession dwelt."[2] She would agree to be his spouse only on condition of his renouncing his false gods. This angers him, and he stirs up her father to wrath. "He promised not ornaments." But as she remained steadfast, her father delivered her over to be put to death, or made to renounce her faith. She still triumphs over all obstacles. In prison the devil appears to her as an angel of light; but a voice from heaven cautions her against him, and tells her to compel him to reveal himself and his doings. Thereupon he tells how he tempts men, and who they are whom he is most likely to succeed with. Such are those who do not make the sign of the Cross. "Some whom I found without God's token—heedless, unblest—these I boldly through diverse deaths with my hands, by my devices, slew."[3] He feels ashamed that he has been conquered by Juliana: "After this sore revenge, I may not laugh at this journey with my comrades, when sad and sorrowing I shall render them my tribute in that

---

[1] Text: *Codex Exoniensis,* edited by B. Thorpe, with translation.
[2] Exeter Book, i., p. 244.
[3] *Ibid.,* v., p. 271.

joyless home." Here is the popular idea of the devil's fear of ridicule, out of which so much has been made in mediæval literature.[1] The MS. is in a mutilated condition. It tells not the whole story. But after many forms of suffering and torments from which Juliana is preserved intact, she is finally beheaded. Then, like a Teuton viking, Heliseus seeks relief from remorse and disappointment in a seafaring life. This part of the poem has the genuine Old English ring :

> "This miscreant, perverse of mind, by ship—
> With him his ruffian band—sought ocean's streams,
> And o'er the water-flood a long while sped;
> But him and his fell band, on the swan-road,
> Ere they to land had steered, did death destroy;
> Of life bereft were four-and-thirty men—
> Whelmed in the raging fury of the waves. . . .
> In that dark home—that den profound—might not
> Their money-gifts apportioned from their prince
> Expect they ; nor in wine-hall, nor on beer-bench,
> Might rings receive with gold embossed."[2]

Thus we find this people still unable to think out of the old routine of thought and life they had lived for centuries. The names are foreign, but the language and the acting and the spirit are all English. After giving his name in Runes the poet begs that every man "who may recite this lay earnestly by my name fervently bear it in mind."

3. Cynewulf sang of the *Last Judgment*.[3] In the allusion to himself, the poet tells his readers that he dreads the doom, "for that I held not well what my Saviour in books commanded me." He exhorts all to be prepared for that day : "Each man should in his course

---

[1] Exeter Book, p. 274. [2] Text: Exeter Book.
[3] *Ibid.*, p. 283.

of years well consider that the Lord of might at first, through the angel's word, came to us benign. Now will he be earnest when he again shall come stern and just." Life he likens to a cruise upon a stormy sea: "It is as though we on the liquid flood in vessels journey; through a wide sea on ocean-horses the flood-wave traverse. That is a perilous stream of boundless waves on which here we are tossed through this weak world— windy seas over a deep path."[1] The poem begins by treating of the destruction of the earth; it then describes the judgment-scene; the Cross is in the heaven a consolation and a hope to the good, a terror to the wicked; then the final sentence is pronounced; and here the Saviour recounts His sufferings on the Holy Rood; finally the respective states of the good and the bad are described.[2] Here is the author's description of the consummation of all things by fire:

So the greedy guest shall earth pervade; the destroying flame shall fill with fire's horror the high structures on the earth's plain; the wide-spreading blast, the whole world together, hot, all-devouring. Down shall fall the city walls, in pieces broken. The hills shall melt; shall melt the high cliffs

[1] Exeter Book, p. 53.
[2] The poem of the *Last Judgment* occupies in the Exeter Book from p. 49 to p. 103. It is usual to assign all the poems, from the beginning to p. 103, to Cynewulf, reading them as one. Thus, Mr. T. Arnold speaks of them as "*Crist*, a long poem on the threefold coming of Christ." (*Manual of English Literature*, 4th ed., p. 14.) I consider the poem of the *Last Judgment* as belonging alone to Cynewulf. The previous poems are more rhapsodical, and seem to have been intended as Church hymns. The style of the *Last Judgment* is of an older flavor. Mythological allusions are more frequent. The imagery is more heathenish. The only artistic fault is the twofold digression on the Rood. The poem, read in this light, seems to me far superior to the author's other known productions. It shows less consciousness of effort.

that erst against ocean, firm against floods, the earth had shielded, stern and steadfast, bulwarks against the waves, the encircling water. Then shall the death-flame seize each creature, beasts and fowls; along the earth shall pass the fire-swart flame, a burning warrior; as of old the rivers, the floods he drove, so then in a fire-bath the sea-fishes shall be burned; cut off from ocean each animal of the wave weary shall die; water shall burn as wax. There shall be more wonders than any may conceive: how the stun,[1] and the storm, and the strong blast shall break broad creation; men shall wail, shall weep, moaning with voices, abject, humble, sad in mind, with repentance afflicted.[2]

Such is the picture the Last Day presented to the imagination of this Old English poet. He speaks of the flame as "a burning warrior" passing along the earth. When Cedmon describes the destruction of Pharaoh and his host in the Red Sea, he represents the guardian of the flood as with one stroke of an ancient falchion striking the unsheltering wave, so "that in the swoon of death the armies slept." Cynewulf lacks the definiteness and the grasp, because he is the lesser poet. But his subjects were popular; he treated them in a popular manner, and therefore was he prized in his own day. His poems are valuable to-day, not as revealing the individual personality of the poet, so much as the common form of poetic thought prevalent in his time. Men think in the forms of their age and their ancestors. That the most prized is a judicious blending of the old with the new. As an instance of this happy blending, take the poet's description of the weeping of the trees when the Redeemer hung upon the Holy Rood:

Yea, the trees also proclaimed who had with branches shaped them when mighty God on one of them ascended, where

[1] *Gestun*, a whirlwind or stun.   [2] Exeter Book, p. 61.

He endured pains for need of earth's inhabitants—a loathly death in help to mortals. Then was many a tree with blood-tears suffused under the heavens; red and thick their sap was turned to gore, so that earth's inhabitants may not say through wise knowledge how many creatures without feeling perceived the Lord's sufferings.

Here is a remembrance of the myth of all nature weeping over the death of Baldr.

IV.—The Poems of Judith and Guthlac, and a Lover's Message.

1. A poem belonging to the same period, and written by a greater genius, is the poem of *Judith*.[1] But we look in vain for the Bible narrative. The heroine is an Englishwoman; Holofernes is an English earl; scenes and incidents are all the scenes and incidents of English life. And that English life is the ideal life of the Old English fancy. It is a picture of war and preparation for war, of feastings that end in brutal drunkenness, of bloody deed and horrid thought. The poem contains an absence of all the elements that would make a poem readable to-day. Still, it is invaluable as a picture of a bygone life. Holofernes gives a feast. "All his fierce chiefs, bold mail-clad warriors, went at the feast to sit, eager to drink wine. There were often carried the deep bowls behind the benches; so likewise vessels and orcas full to those sitting at supper. . . . Then was Holofernes rejoiced with wine; in the halls of his guests he laughed and shouted, he roared and dinned. Afar off might the stern one be heard to storm and clamor. . . . So was the wicked one—the lord and his men—drunk with wine, . . . till that they swimming lay . . . as

---

[1] Text: 1. Grimm's *Judith*; 2. Thorpe's *Analecta Anglo-Saxonica*. See also Turner's *Hist. Anglo-Saxons*, iii., ch. iii., p. 309.

they were death-slain. . . ." We confine the description to the most salient points. The repetitions are meaningless without the alliteration in which they are expressed, and then they become emphatic. Holofernes, overcome with drink, in stupor lies on his bed. Then Judith accomplishes the deed that is to deliver Israel. The poet goes into the minutest details:

> She took the heathen man fast by his hair; she drew him by his limbs toward her disgracefully; and the mischief-full, odious man, at her pleasure laid, so as the wretch she might the easiest well command. She with the twisted locks struck the hateful enemy, meditating hate, with the red sword, till she had half cut off his neck; so that he lay in a swoon, drunk and mortally wounded. He was not then dead—not entirely lifeless; earnest then she struck another time the heathen hound—she the woman illustrious in strength—till that his head rolled forth upon the floor. Cofferless lay the foul one; downward turned his spirit under the abyss, and there was plunged below with sulphur fastened; for ever afterward wounded by worms. In torments bound—hard imprisoned—he burns in hell. After his course he need not hope that he may escape from that mansion of worms, with darkness overwhelmed; but there he shall remain ever and ever—without end—henceforth void of the joys of hope, in that cavern home.

Judith returns to the city with the head of this wicked one. She is met by the people, and orders them to prepare for battle: "Now, I beseech every man of these citizens, these shield-warriors, that ye immediately haste you to fight. When God, the source of all, the honor-fast king, from the east sends a ray of light, bring forth your banners; with shields for your breasts and mails for your hams, go ye among the robbers; let their leaders fall, the devoted chiefs, by the ruddy sword." We need not give the description of battle. It is the stereotyped one. We have the usual accompaniments—the wolf, the raven, the kite, the eagle, the song of the sword, the stern-mindedness, and the fierce hate. "Stern-minded, they advanced with fierce spirits; they pressed on unsoftly, with ancient hate, against the mead-weary foe." The poem, as we now have it, is a mere fragment. But it is characteristic of the English mind, and reveals not a few glimpses of genius.

2. Another, and more agreeable though less powerful poem, is that on *St. Guthlac.* It reveals a distinct order of thought. With the poet, the spiritual and the physical worlds are intimately united. Earth and heaven and hell all touch one another. Angels and demons quarrel over human souls. He who lives with his hand ever knocking at heaven's door, and hell beneath his feet, and saints and spirits around him, takes a far different view of life from him who looks upon it as a state in which to take all the joys and pleasures within his reach. Such was Guthlac. The saving of his soul was the one object for which he lived. And, that it shall not be damned through his intercourse with men, he abandons all and retires to a lone spot, there to lead a hermit-life. This happens to be a resting-place for demons. No welcome guest is the holy man among them. They threaten him; they torment him; they promise him all manner of goods if he only leaves them this solitary spot. But all to no purpose. Guthlac is steadfast. The fiends bear him hither and thither. St. Bartholomew comes to his assistance and compels them to bear him back to the hill whence they took him. And then we are told: "The feathered tribe made known the holy man's return; oft had he held them food, when hungry they flew round his hand. . . . Serene was the glorious plain and his new dwelling; sweet the birds' song, the earth flowery; cuckoos announced the year."

This blending of description of nature with the narrative is a new feature in Old English poetry. We do not find it in any of the earlier productions. Nowhere do we read that earth or sea welcomed the hero or was glad at his coming. It is Christianity that sheds that gentle light upon nature, and brings it into sympathy with human feelings. However, if the poem has this modern excellency, it also, and in excess, possesses the modern defect of moralizing. Again, disease strikes the saint. His disciple becomes alarmed: "Then was wail and sighing to the youth, his spirit sad, his soul grieving, when he heard that the holy man was on departure bent." Guthlac grows worse: "Death drew nigh, stepped with iron strides, strong and fierce sought the soul-house." Finally, on the last day, the saint gives this message to his disciple. It is a beautiful thought, that only Christianity could have created; and it is touching as it is beautiful: "Go tell my sister, the most beloved, my departure on a long way to the fair joy, to an eternal dwelling; and eke make known to her that at all times in this life I denied myself her presence, in order that we may again see each other sinless before the face of the Eternal Judge, where our love shall continue faithful, and we may ever enjoy our wishes in the bright city." This is the language of a strong mind, holding his soul in his hands, and resolved that not even a sisterly affection shall go between him and his God.

3. We have one other instance in Old English poetry in which man sends a message to woman. It is not such a heavenly message as that of St. Guthlac. It may be older than his, but its Runic character places it no later than the present period. We have but a fragment of the poem to which it belongs. We will call it *The*

Lover's Message.[1] It is the story of one driven from his home by feuds: "Him feuds drove away from the noble people." He builds up for himself another home in foreign lands. And he remembers her in whom his affections are centered. He sends a messenger to her with a Runic token, asking her to come and live with him. The fragment represents the messenger pressing his friend's suit. He describes his wealth; he tells her that she alone is lacking to complete his happiness; he assures her that his friend is prepared to fulfill the promises which they in early days oft spake: "Yes, he who inscribed this beam bade me beseech thee that thou, richly-adorned one, shouldst bethink thee in thy mind's recess the promises which ye two in early days oft spake, when one land ye did inhabit, and while ye might in the mead-burghs foster friendship. . . . He now bids thee gladly learn to brave the water, when on the mountain's brow thou hast heard the cuckoo's mournful song in the grove." The tradition of calling the cuckoo's lay a sad one is old. We are unable to gather from the poem whether the woman's affection was as steadfast as that of the man. Be this as it may, the poem is unique in the history of Old English literature. It is the only fragment giving us the story of man's love for woman. It betrays an absence of passion and chivalry. There is no sentiment—no impulse leading the lover to risk his life for this object of his affections; while he expects her to abandon herself to the mercy of the sea for his sake. All this is in accordance with what we have seen to be the Old English idea of marriage.

[1] It is found on page 473 of the Exeter Book.

CHAPTER VI.

JARROW AND YORK.

I.—BENEDICT BISCOP.

WITH Theodore was BENEDICT BISCOP. He was a zealous promoter of the new learning and the new creed. He made no less than five journeys to Rome. Each journey he brought back with him some boon or other to his countrymen. Now it was some valuable books; again some skilled workingmen and artificers; at another time it was beautiful paintings. At first he taught the school at Canterbury, but resigned in favor of Adrian. He then built the monasteries of Wearmouth and Jarrow. He initiated the English into many improved ways. He inaugurated a better style of architecture. Instead of the thatched roof, he made use of lead. He brought over from France masons and glass-makers, whose skill was the admiration of the less cultivated English. And with the great comfort of light and protection from the weather, introduced by the use of glass, he undertook to educate their æsthetic sense. They who formerly had no other use for color than to paint their shields now had opportunity, through the considerate kindness of Benedict, of looking upon paintings of sacred subjects. And though the primary object was, as we are told, that all, however ignorant, might contemplate as through a veil the countenance of

Christ and his saints, and so be moved to piety, still those paintings improved the tastes of the people. He even pleased the taste of King Aldfred by bringing him two cloaks of silk, for which in return he received three hundred and sixty acres of land. Nor did Benedict stop here. He also brought from Rome John the Chanter, to teach the Gregorian music. The ceremonies of religion grew more attractive, and the people flocked in crowds to listen to the new music, and be moved by its solemn harmony. The monks of Wearmouth grew famous for their good singing; those from other monasteries flocked thither to be instructed by this celebrated teacher. "The said John," says Beda, "not only taught the brothers of that monastery, but such as had skill in singing resorted from almost all the monasteries in the same province to hear him, and many invited him to teach in other places."[1] Thus it was that while Theodore was ministering to men's souls and Adrian to their intellects, Benedict Biscop was cultivating their tastes; but in the hands of all three, art and philosophy and letters and doctrine were the handmaids of piety and religion. Benedict died in the monastery of Wearmouth. On his death-bed his last charge was to guard with care the treasures of the noble and rich library he had brought from Rome.[2] And one was there who placed those treasures out at usurious interest, and with them gained the wherewith to enrich his own and succeeding ages. That one is he who has recorded the facts here related—the Venerable Beda.

II.—BEDA.

BEDA (672–735) was born on the property of the Wearmouth Monastery. At the age of seven, he was

[1] *Eccl. Hist.*, b. iv., ch. 18.   [2] *Ibid.*

placed in charge of Benedict Biscop. Under this good man's guidance he grew up, knowing little of the world, and learning less of its rudeness, its evil ways, and bad examples. And as he advanced in years, and his intellect matured, he became the light and model of his community. From Wearmouth he was transferred to Jarrow, where he passed the remainder of his life. In his own beautifully simple style he tells us the story of that life : "And spending all the remaining time of my life in that monastery, I wholly applied myself to the study of Scripture, and amid the observance of regular discipline, and the daily care of singing in the church, I always took delight in learning, teaching, and writing." This is the simple summary of his life. It speaks of a life of retirement and prayer ; it reveals a monk seldom leaving his monastery for any length of time except to make an occasional excursion in search of materials for his numerous works. And yet there was no subject beneath his notice or beyond his grasp. In his twenty-seventh year, and while still a deacon, he is already so famous that Pope Sergius calls him to Rome.[1] Such honors disturb not the even tenor of his life. He continues his labors in the schoolroom with all the zeal of an apostle. He numbers no less than six hundred pupils who gather round him to receive some share of his great learning. He composes text-books for their use on mathematics, on physics, on astronomy, on grammar, on rhetoric, on dialectics, on meteorology, on music and medicine ; he writes commentaries on the sacred Scriptures after the manner of Gregory the Great, which are still quoted with approval ; he translates portions of the Bible into his mother-tongue ; he composes pious hymns for the people to sing ; he writes the lives of many of

[1] William of Malmesbury.

the great and good men in the English Church who went before him; he records the struggles and trials and triumphs of Christianity among his people, and their advance in the road of civilization. He is the living encyclopædia of his age. His knowledge embraces all that time has left of Greek and Roman civilizations. He stands out the greatest intellect in the whole range of the Old English period. The guiding principle of his life is a sincere love for truth in all shapes and under all aspects. He is no dreamer. He lives and works for the present, and therefore it is that his name has passed into the future. Nor is his eye always on books. He casts an occasional glance upon affairs of church and state. He exhorts Ecgberht, Archbishop of York, in his duties; he calls his attention to the spiritual wants of the faithful living in remote districts; he denounces those monks who seem to have no other intention of entering a monastery than to escape military service; he regards the wants of the kingdom with all the knowingness of a veteran statesman, and becomes indignant over those who under pretense of piety would defraud Cæsar out of his own.[1]

His love for truth will not allow him to rest even in sickness. Not long before his death, and when he should have had complete repose, we find him preparing text-books for his dear pupils: "I will not have my pupils," said he, "read a falsehood, nor labor therein without profit."[2] He is only too happy that he is able to work. What he can do for himself, he lets not others do for him. "I am my own secretary," he writes; "I make my own notes; I am my own librarian." His truth-loving spirit penetrates all the sciences and extracts

[1] Epist. ii., "Ad Ecgberctum Antistitem," *Opera*, t. v., p. 658, ed. Migne. [2] Letter of Cuthberht.

from them whatever it found good and useful. His scientific knowledge is the most accurate his times afford. Still, as might be expected, some of his explanations are childlike; others erroneous; nor can he rid himself altogether of the superstitions of the day. He believes the comet to portend change of kingdoms, or pestilence, or war, or tempest, or drought.[1] On the other hand, when he undertakes to explain the theory of the tides, he rises far above the crude notions of his times, and almost anticipates Newton.[2]

But the masterpiece of Beda is his *Ecclesiastical History of the English Nation*. It was for him a labor of love, although it took some persuasion to prevail upon him to begin it. His friends Albinus and Acca, the Bishop of Hexham, encouraged him. But once he undertook the task, he spared no pains. He was indefatigable in his researches. Northelm, a learned priest, brings him from Rome the important correspondence between Augustin and Pope Gregory the Great. He gathers the traditions of the pious and learned missionaries who first came among the English people, and sifts them carefully. He converses with eye-witnesses of events and weighs their statements. He everywhere brings to bear upon his narrative the great good sense that characterizes him. "Thus much of the Ecclesiastical History of Britain," says he, "and more especially of the English nation, as far as I could learn either from the writings of the ancients, or the traditions of our ancestors, or of my own knowledge, has, with the help of God, been digested by me, Beda, the servant of God and priest of the Monastery of the Blessed Apostles Peter and Paul, which is at Wearmouth and Jarrow."[3] It is not, therefore, fair to tax

[1] *De Nat. Rerum.* [2] *Ibid.* [3] *Ecclesiastical History*, at the end.

him with credulity. The marvelous and the legendary that he records were searchingly probed, and he only gave that which he regarded as the most probable. His was a simple faith that no amount of learning could cloud, and that saw in the material as well as in the spiritual world the interposition of Divine Providence. And not only does he write with deep earnestness; his is the pen of an artist as well. His soul glows with the poet's enthusiasm over the description of a favorite theme, and the narrative of a good deed or a good life. Sometimes it bursts forth into a hymn of praise, as when, after speaking of the miraculous preservation of the body of Queen Etheldrida, he sings:

"Triumphing joy attends the peaceful soul,
When heat, nor rain, nor wishes mean control.
Thus Etheldrida, pure from sensual crime,
Bright shining star! arose to bless our time." [1]

Such was the historian, whose veracity has never been questioned. We can not imagine him distorting a fact for his own private purposes, or coloring a narrative in order to bear out a preconceived notion. He was innocent of the tricks of modern historians. To question his sincerity were to prove one's self ignorant of the man.

The story of his death is well known. It has been beautifully told by his disciple Cuthberht. He who so lovingly lingered over the death of England's first great Christian poet, found one to give a touching account of his own. And, as we have described the one, let us watch the departure of England's ripest scholar and greatest historian. The story is too beautiful and too instructive not to repeat. He had been ailing about two months. Still he worked hard, teaching his numerous disciples and composing books for them. Withal he re-

[1] Translation in Smith's *Bede*.

tained his cheerful disposition. But daily he grew worse, and his disciples, with heavy heart, saw his last hour approach. Death comes and still finds him at work. He is translating the Gospel of St. John into his mother-speech. The morning of his last day dawns. "There is still another chapter wanting, and it is hard for thee to question thyself any longer," said an eager pupil when he saw his master's extreme weakness. "It is easily done," said the holy man. "Take thy pen and write quickly." And painfully he dictated the words, his voice growing weaker and weaker. He rests a moment. "Dear master, there is yet one sentence unwritten," said the pupil. "Write it quickly," said Beda, for he felt his strength ebbing fast. "It is finished now," said the pupil. "You say truly," replied the dying man, "it is finished. Hold my head in your hands, for I desire to sit facing the holy place in which I was wont to pray." After praying for some time, his poet nature burst forth in a song in his own tongue on the uncertain lot of a departed soul. "Being learned in our poetry," says Cuthberht, "he said some things also in our speech, for he said, putting the same in English":

Fore the neidfæræ	Before the necessary journey
nenig uniurthit	no one is
thonc-snotturra	wiser of thought
than him tharf sie,	than he hath need,
to ymbhycgannæ	to consider
ær his hiniongæ,	before his departure,
huat his gastae	what for his spirit
godaes æththe yflæs	of good or evil
æfter deoth-daege	after the death-day
doemid unieorthæ.	shall be doomed.[1]

[1] This version of Beda's sole surviving words in his mother-speech, is taken by J. M. Kemble from the MS. at St. Gall. He gives it with

Finally he rendered his pure soul into the hands of his Creator, while in the act of singing the praises of the Holy Trinity. So passed away the glory of his day.

We are now dealing with the golden age of Old English scholarship. Ecgberht was making of York a worthy rival of Wearmouth and Yarrow and Canterbury. Northumbria was becoming classic ground. To this period especially apply the words of Professor Maurice: "Schools seem to rise as by enchantment; all classes down to the poorest (Beda himself is the obvious example) are admitted to them; the studies, beginning from theology, embrace logic, rhetoric, music, astronomy."[1] We have seen how Beda completes this system by adding to it physics, medicine, meteorology, and other branches. And not only were men versed in learning; we find women versed as well. We have seen that Aldhelm writes his treatise in praise of virginity in Latin, for a community of nuns. Boniface corresponds with English ladies in Latin. Leobgitha asks him concerning some verses she composed on the Creator— "according to the discipline of poetic tradition"— which discipline she learned from the teacher of Eadburga.[2] In fact, it would seem that the clergy were neglecting their mother-speech in their devotedness to the language of the Church. In the Council of Cliff, held in 747, twelve years after the death of Beda, and presided over by St. Cuthberht, King Ethelbald being present, it was decreed that every priest should know how to explain in his mother-tongue the creed, the

translation in *Archæologia*, vol. xxviii. The student of Old English will notice the peculiarities of the Northumbrian dialect, such as æ for e, and even for o in the word *æththe*. The fragment is a precious relic.

[1] *Philosophy in the First Six Centuries.*
[2] Epist. 21, Leobgitha Bonifacio, A. D. 725.

Lord's prayer, the words used in celebrating the holy mysteries, administering baptism, and the other offices of the Church; and it was imposed upon those who knew not how to interpret and explain in their own tongue, to learn.[1]

III.—ALCWIN.

From Jarrow we pass to York. ECGBERHT is the brother of the King of Northumbria. He is also Archbishop of York. But his greatest honor is to have been a pupil of Beda's. He brings to York the traditions of Jarrow. His admiration for his great master leads him to imitate his manner of teaching. His daily life has been handed down to us. It differs from ours, and for that reason is all the more instructive: "He rose at daybreak, and, when he was not prevented by more important occupations, sitting on his couch, taught his pupils successively till noon. He then retired to his chapel and celebrated mass.[2] At the time of dinner, he repaired to the common hall, where he ate sparingly, though he was careful that the meat should be of the best kind. During dinner a book of instruction was always read. Till the evening he amused himself with hearing his scholars discuss literary subjects. Then he repeated with them the service of complin, called them to him, and, as they successively knelt before him, gave them his benediction. They afterward retired to rest."[3] Among the pupils so taught was Alcwin. He extends the influence of Jarrow and York to the Continent.

[1] "Interpretari atque exponere posse propria lingua, qui nesciant, discant." (*Conc. Cloveshoviense*, Wilkins, vol. i., p. 95.)

[2] "Sanctificabat eos, offerens corpus Christi et sanguinem pro omnibus." (*Vita Alc.*, p. 149.)

[3] Lingard, *Anglo-Saxon Antiquities*, p. 207. These details Alcwin used to relate to his friends.

ALCWIN.

ALCWIN (735-804), from his youth, was devoted to learning both sacred and profane. Charlemagne prevailed upon him to reside at his court, there to establish schools and assist him in the educational reform he was then digesting for his subjects. Alcwin entered upon his new duties with energy. He opened a school in the palace, which was attended by the Emperor and the principal persons of his household. He revived schools throughout the kingdom. He took all possible means to encourage study. He revised, corrected, and restored ancient manuscripts. His labors extended even to the plays of Terence, which he copied.[1] Thus he encouraged the classics, but he made them subservient to sacred studies. He exhorted his disciples to study " for God, for purity of soul, for the knowing of truth, even for one's self ; but not for mere human praise, or worldly honors, or even the false pleasures of riches."[2] The whole of France wakened to a new life under his influence. Men threw off the intellectual sloth in which they had been living, and devoted themselves with ardor to learning. " Under Alcwin's direction," says a cautious writer, " a scheme of education was drawn up which became the model for the other great schools established at Tours, Fontenelle, Lyons, Osnaburg, and Metz—institutions which ably sustained the tradition of education on the Continent, until superseded by the new methods and the new learning which belong to the commencement of the University era.[3] He had some of his pupils sent to York to take copies of the literary treasures there kept. And they brought with them,

---

[1] Guizot, *Histoire de la France*, t. ii., p. 187.
[2] Apud Lingard, p. 192.
[3] J. B. Mullinger, *The University of Cambridge from the Earliest Times to the Royal Injunctions of* 1535, p. 13.

not only the works, but also the beautiful style of illuminating practiced at this time in England. This style for centuries afterward characterized a special school of illuminators on the Continent.[1]

Alcwin was by nature an ascetic; but he was also a courtier, a scholar, and an educator.[2] He was above all a devoted child of the Church. He fought the errors of the day with vigor; he wrote commentaries on the sacred Scriptures; he prepared a moral treatise on vice and virtue. His finger may be traced in the *Capitularies* of Charlemagne. He writes to that monarch in behalf of the barbarians he has brought under subjection, showing him the easiest and most effective means of converting them to Catholicity. As a writer, Alcwin was too steeped in classical learning not to compose with a certain correctness; but his style is not admired for its ease and grace, though, like Erasmus—like all mediæval and modern polished Latinists using a language out of their thinking—he often lays more stress upon manner than upon matter. He was not an original thinker. His merit consists in knowing how to make the most of the writings at his command. In his philosophical works he drew largely from St. Augustine.[3] In his educational treatises he made use of

[1] "It has been said that the manuscripts which Alcwin procured from England were the means of forming a special school of transcribers and illuminators at Aix-la-Chapelle, which for many generations preserved the traditional style of the Anglo-Saxon artists." (Edwards, *Memoirs of Libraries*.)

[2] "C'est un moine, un diacre, la lumière de l'Église contemporaine; mais c'est en même temps un érudit, un lettré classique." (Guizot, *Civilisation en France*, lect. xxii., p. 208.)

[3] "Alcwin had in his hands some glosses of Boëthius, the works of the condensers Cassiodorus, Isidore of Seville, and the poetic manual of Martianus Capella. Now, there is nothing in his *Dialectics* which

the Compendiums of Beda. But he was painstaking and methodical; and these are essential qualities for a good educator. It is as an educator that he has most interest for us. He brought his methods from England, and these methods continued to be used in France and Germany long after his death. There has been preserved to us a dialogue between Alcwin and Pepin. No doubt it is a specimen of the literary conversations that were of daily occurrence in the palace school. And these in their turn were modeled after those in which Alcwin himself had been exercised by Archbishop Ecgberht. The dialogue is simple, but it belongs to a simple age. The comforts of a court—even of the court of Charlemagne—were inferior to those enjoyed at present by a family merely above want. In the *Capitularies* of Charlemagne are prescriptions relative to the chickens of his barnyard, and the sale of eggs and vegetables.[1] This is patriarchal primitiveness.

IV.—Popular Philosophy.

1. And so in the efforts to solve the mysteries of nature, of life and death, of thought and affection, we must look for simple questions and silly answers. Still, these questions of Alcwin are invaluable as giving us the level of the popular intelligence on the ever-recurring problems that suggest themselves to the human mind,

---

is not found in these works and in the treatise on the Ten Categories: he only abridged abridgments." (Hauréau, *Philosophie Scholastique*, i., p. 105.) Hauréau shows rare acuteness in tracing ideas to their source; but in justice to Alcwin let us add that these abridgments embodied the whole literary tradition of the past. Possessing them was possessing nearly all the available knowledge of the eighth century.

[1] Cantù, *Histoire Universelle*, t. vii., p. 372.

and to which it must have an answer, be it right or wrong. Pepin asks Alcwin, and is answered in the following manner:

"What is writing?" "The guardian of History."
"What is speech?" "The interpreter of the soul."
"What is it that gives birth to speech?" "The tongue."
"What is the tongue?" "The whip of the air."
"What is the air?" "The preserver of life."
"What is life?" "A joy for the happy, a pain for the miserable, the expectation of death."
"What is death?" "An inevitable event, an uncertain voyage, a subject of tears for the living, the confirmation of testaments, the robber of men. . . ."
"What is heaven?" "A moving sphere, an immense vault."
"What is light?" "The torch of all things."
"What is the day?" "A call to labor."
"What is the sun?" "The splendor of the universe, the beauty of the firmament, the grace of nature, the glory of the day, the distributor of the hours. . . ."
"What is friendship?" "The similarity of souls. . . ."
"As you are a youth of good disposition, and endowed with natural capacity, I will put to you several other unusual questions: endeavor to solve them."
"I will do my best; if I make mistakes, you must correct them."
"I shall do as you desire. Some one who is unknown to me has conversed with me, having no tongue and no voice; he was not before, he will not be hereafter, and I neither heard nor knew him. What means this?"
"Perhaps a dream moved you, master?"
"Exactly so, my son. Still another one. I have seen the dead engender the living, and the dead consumed by the breath of the living."
"Fire was born from the rubbing of branches, and it consumed the branches."[1]

[1] Guizot, *Histoire de la Civilisation en France*, t. ii., p. 191.

2. Such was the kind of information that satisfied Alcwin and pleased Pepin. Nor was it so with these alone. It was that on which the common intelligence lived in England as well as in France and Italy. Nations have their periods of intellectual childhood as well as individuals. They are as inquisitive as children, and like children rest content with apparent solutions. They delight in riddles and enigmas. The priest SIGULF writes a catechism on the events related in the Bible. It is written in the language of the people. The solutions show lack of imagination and a degree of intelligence that could not rise far above its swine and its oxen. Here are specimens: "8. 'Why did the Creator curse the earth on Adam's guilt, and not the water?' 'Because God's command to man concerned the earth's fruits, not the water's; and because God remembered that by means of water he would destroy the sin that man drew upon himself through the earth's fruit.'" The priest here alludes to the water of baptism, and in writing that answer he evidently forgot the reasons for blessing the water so used. Here is another: "30. 'Why was the tree by which Adam fell called *lignum scientiæ boni et mali*, that is in English, tree of the knowledge of good and evil?' 'It was not because the tree was intelligent in its kind, nor that it knew good and evil; but in order that man might know from the tree that was forbidden him how much good is in obedience and how much evil in disobedience.'" The reader will remember Cædmon's description of the two trees, one of good and one of evil. Men have been two centuries learning Christianity since then. Again, here are some questions on the rainbow: "53. 'Why was the rainbow set as a pledge to mankind?' 'God set the rainbow as a pledge and safety to man,*

for a promise that He never after would cover the earth with a flood; for He knew if He did not, that men through fear would anticipate a similar flood every time they saw such rains.'" This answer gives the substance of the Scripture text. "54. 'Why is that token seen in the clouds of heaven?' 'That all men may see it, and that we be reminded in every trouble to turn our thoughts to God who dwelleth in heaven.' 55. 'Why is the token of various colors?' 'On the token is the hue of water and of fire; that token that is the rainbow comes of the sunbeam and of wet clouds in order that the earth may be safe: it has the water's color, that water may not drown us all and that we may conquer it; it has the fire's color, that all this world may be kindled with fire on the great day.'"[1] So the questions run. It is noteworthy that the English catechisms all refer to Bible and religious subjects. The craving of the English mind in that direction seems insatiable. Not satisfied with the sparks itself strikes out, it adopts the views of other peoples on the same or like subjects. And so we find all other questionings thrown in the shade by the popular series called *Salomon and Saturn*.

3. This work comes we know not whence. It is a strange conglomeration of all lores. We open the leaves and hit upon this passage: "Lo! I have learned that in days of yore men wise of mood—princes of the earth—contended, struggled about their wisdom. Ill doth he that lieth or the truth rejecteth."[2] Meeting these words we are prepared to assign it a Northern origin. We find a continuation of the Scandinavian sagas wherein men staked their lives on the answering of a question

---

[1] MSS. Cott., Jul. E. vii., fol. 228.
[2] *Salomon and Saturn*, edited by J. M. Kemble for the Ælfric Society, part i., p. 154.

or the solving of a riddle. The groundwork is of a piece with the old heathen sagas. But we go back a few pages, and wonder if we are not reading a homily from one of the Early Fathers. Hear how the word of God is spoken of: "Golden is the word of God, and stoned with gems; it hath silver leaves; . . . it is wisdom of the breast and honey of the soul; it is milk of the mind, most blessed of glories." And this Christian element in it is entirely foreign to the English mind. It bears the impress of an Eastern cast of thought. Such is the peculiar treatment of the Pater-noster. Every letter and every word in it has each its peculiar virtue. None is more powerful than the Pater-noster. "Saturn spake: But who may easiest of all creatures the holy door of heaven's kingdom bright unclose in succession? Salomon quoth: The palm-twigged Pater-noster openeth the heavens, blesseth the holy, maketh mild the Lord, pulleth down murder, quencheth the devil's fire, kindleth the Lord's: thus mayst thou . . . with the bright prayer heat the blood of the devil's wizard, so that in him the drops shall rise hurried with blood in the thoughts of his breast, more full of terror than the brazen caldron, when it for twelve generations of men most greedily bubbleth."[1] And with the Christian, there is also a pagan Orientalism. Such is the doctrine that fire is the origin of all things: "For there is no kind of thing that lives, nor bird, nor fish, nor stone of the earth, nor water's wave, nor twig of wood, nor mount, nor moor, nor even this earth, but what it cometh forth from a kind of fire."[2] We have seen how the cross was venerated by the English people. From an early day,

[1] *Salomon and Saturn*, p. 145.

[2] *Ibid.*, p. 170. This doctrine was also taught by Heraclitus. And Hooker (*Eccl. Polity*, b. i., § ii.) attributes it to the Stoics. But it originated, perhaps, in Chaldea.

men signed themselves with the saving sign. Tertullian tells us the practice was common among the primitive Christians. In *Salomon and Saturn,* the man's body not so signed was in the power of the devil: "And when the devil is very weary he seeketh the cattle of some sinful man, or an unclean tree; or if he meeteth the mouth and body of a man that hath not been blessed, then goeth he into the bowels of a man who has so forgotten, and through his skin, and through his flesh, departeth into the earth, and from these findeth his way into hell's desert."[1] And a question that seemed to have special interest for English curiosity was that asking the various ingredients of which Adam's body was composed by his Creator. This, also, is solved in a prose version of this mysterious book: "'Tell me the substance of which Adam, the first man, was made.' 'I tell thee of eight pounds by weight.' 'Tell me what they are called.' 'I tell thee the first was a pound of earth, of which his flesh was made; the second was a pound of fire, whence his blood came red and hot; the third was a pound of wind, and thence his breathing was given to him; the fourth was a pound of the welkin, thence was his unsteadiness of mood given him; the fifth was a pound of grace—*gyfepund*—whence was given him his growth; the sixth was a pound of blossoms, whence was given him the variety of his eyes; the seventh was a pound of dew, whence he got his sweat; the eighth was a pound of salt, and thence were his tears salt."[2] This was taught and implicitly believed for centuries.[3]

---

[1] *Salomon and Saturn,* p. 149.   [2] *Ibid.,* p. 149.

[3] The same question and answer are found in *The Maisters of Oxford's Catechism,* which is written in fifteenth-century English. The only variation is that occurring in the fifth, which reads: "Of air, where-thorough he speketh and thinketh." (*Ibid.,* p. 217.)

And not only in England, but throughout the Continent of Europe did *Salomon and Saturn*, under diverse names and in diverse forms, mold the maxims of the people.[1]

4. But back of all books, in the Aryan family, is a common fund of wisdom bought from experience. The oldest collection of such sayings in Old English is to be found in the Exeter Book. The editor, Benjamin Thorpe, has headed it *Gnomic Verses*.[2] Many of them are commonplaces and truisms. Others of them give insight into Old English thought. We are told, "Skillful men should in proverbs commune." This is a traditional saying from the old Scandinavian mythology, and by the ordinary English intelligence of that day more honored, we fear, in the breach than in the observance. Some of the sayings are based upon custom, as this one: "The earl shall be magnificent in horses and geldings, and in always and everywhere bestowing mead upon his friends." Some, again, are generalized from experience, as this one referring to the choosing of worthy companions: "A friendless unhappy man takes wolves for his comrades; a much crafty beast, the comrade full often tears him; there shall be horror for the gray one." Or instance this one upon the gadding woman: "A rambling woman scatters words; she is often charged with faults; a man thinks of her with contempt; oft her cheek he smites." These are all of a piece with what we have learned of the Old English character. But we have found the people to be a home-loving people. And so one of the most touching and beautiful verses in this collection alludes to the comfort

[1] This influence has been traced with great learning and industry in the version of *Salomon and Saturn* which Kemble prepared for the Ælfric Society in 1848.
[2] Exeter Book, pp. 333–346.

the sailor experiences when he reaches home: "Dear to the Frisian wife is the welcome guest, when the vessel strands; his ship is come, and her husband to his house, her own provider. And she welcomes him in, washes his weedy garment, and clothes him with new raiment. 'Tis pleasant on shore to him whom his love awaits."[1] And the mention of the Frisian wife points to its antiquity. It was a reminder in the new homestead for the Englishman to seek his wife among his own people. Tacitus tells us of the exclusiveness of the Germanic tribes, and their aversion to intermarriage with other races.

V.—THE REFLECTIVE MOOD IN POETRY.

1. We are now arrived at a new phase of English thought. We have seen the English mind compare life to the flight of a bird—in at one door and out at another, whence it came and whither it went being equally unknown to the lookers-on; we have found death in its thought to be a passing to the halls of Valhalla, there to lead a life of riot and mead-drinking. Now that same mind stops at the grave. It has learned to distinguish between body and soul. It considers what is to come of that body after death. It is such a mood that inspires this mournful poem called *The Grave:*

> "For thee was a house built
> Ere thou wert born;
> For thee was a mold meant
> Ere thou of mother camest.
> But it is not made ready,
> Nor its depth measured,
> Nor is it seen
> How long it shall be.
> Now I bring thee

[1] Exeter Book, *Gnomic Verses*, p. 389.

Where thou shalt be,
And I shall measure thee
And the mold afterward. . . .

"Doorless is that house,
And dark it is within;
There thou art fast detained,
And Death hath the key.
Loathsome is that earth-house,
And grim within to dwell,
And worms shall divide thee.

"Thus thou art laid,
And leavest thy friends;
Thou hast no friend
Who will come to thee,
Who will ever see
How that house pleaseth thee,
Who will ever open
The door for thee,
And descend after thee;
For soon thou art loathsome
And hateful to see."[1]

2. And as English thought was pleased to contemplate the grave, so it makes the soul haunt it even after death. The last journey of the soul was a long and serious affair. Within the first seven nights after death the soul was supposed to visit the body, and praise or blame it according to its apprehensions of a favorable or unfavorable judgment. For according to Old English thinking the soul had to pass three hundred years before its lot was finally decided upon. This belief gives rise to *The Soul's Complaint to the Body* :

"Befits it well that man should deeply weigh
His soul's last journey; how he then may fare

[1] Longfellow's translation. The text is in the Exeter Book.

When death comes on him, and breaks short in twain
The bond that held his flesh and spirit linked:
Long is it thence ere at the hands of Heaven
The spirit shall reap joy or punishment,
E'en as she did in this her earthly frame.
For ere the seventh night of death hath past,
Ghastly and shrieking shall that spirit come—
The soul to find its body.—Restless thus
(Unless high Heaven first work the end of all things)
A hundred years thrice told the shade shall roam."[1]

Here is evidently a trace of the Hindu and Egyptian doctrine of the transmigration of souls. It is one of the modes of accounting for the existence of ghosts. It shows the persistency with which the English mind asked for a solution of the riddle beyond the grave.

3. A still later poem, which has been added to the Old English poetical calendar, called *Menology*, repeats the uncertainty of Beda upon the future condition of man's soul. It speaks almost despondingly: "The future condition is dark and secret; the Lord—the Redeeming Father—only knows. No one returns hither under roofs, who here may reveal to men for certain what is the condition of the Creator, what the glorious habitation of people where He himself dwells."[2] Such are the views of death this people has handed down to us. They are grave and solemn. They are congenial to its naturally serious thinking. A people to which war is a play, whose delight is in danger, and which has

---

[1] *The Soul's Complaint to the Body*, Conybeare's translation; text, Exeter Book.

[2] *Menology*, edition of Rev. S. Fox, p. 55. The verses added to the calendar proper are evidently by another hand. When Mr. Fox compares them to a Pindaric Ode, he allows his admiration to run away with his judgment.

forgotten the halls of Valhalla, must needs question intensely what lies beyond the grave.[1]

4. There is a fragment called *The Ruin*. It reveals rare poetical power. It was evidently written by a true child of song. But it is not, as has been suggested, of a pre-insular date. The rude child of the forest knew not the use of stone buildings, his eye was not familiarized to tower and battlement and steepled splendor. All this he learned later. But all this is found in the fragment. The poet is meditative in presence of the ruins. He remembers the mighty ones who once dwelt there. He contrasts its present with its former condition:

Wondrous is this wall-stone, the fates have broken it — have burst the burgh-place. Perishes the work of giants; fallen are the roofs, the towers tottering—the hoar gate-towers despoiled—rime on the lime—*hrim on lime;* shattered are the battlements, riven, fallen under the Eotnish race; the earth-grave has its powerful workmen; decayed, departed, the hard of gripe are fallen and passed away to a hundred generations of people. . . . Bright were the burgh-dwellings, many its princely halls, high its steepled splendor; there was martial sound great, many a mead-hall full of human joys, until obdurate fate changed it all; they perished in wide slaughter. . . . There many a chief of old, joyous and gold-bright, splendidly decorated, proud, and with wine elate, in warlike decorations shone; looked on treasures, on silver, on

---

[1] The *Dialogue between the Soul and the Body* was very popular throughout the middle ages in every country in Europe. Wright mentions versions in twelve different languages. In his edition of the *Latin Poems commonly attributed to Walter Mapes*, edited for the Camden Society (1841), he prints a Latin version, one in Anglo-Norman, and two in thirteenth-century English. But none of them is as early as the Old English version; and it is no rash conclusion to say that it is the suggester of the Latin version first, and through it of all the others.

curious gems, on luxury, on wealth, on precious stone, on this bright burgh of a broad realm.¹

Thus it is that this reflective mood extends itself not only to death, but to everything suggestive of death. This intense seriousness is the largest trait of Old English thought. If at this stage it is not productive of more fruitful results, it is because the Old English mind is slow in its movements.

¹ Exeter Book, pp. 476-78.

CHAPTER VII.

WINCHESTER.

ANOTHER night of ignorance settled upon England. The lights that issued from Jarrow and York became extinguished in the ruins of these noble monasteries. The Danes came, and during the greater part of the ninth century pillaged churches, depopulated cities, outraged monk and nun, and brought in their trail misery and barbarism. Their fury was especially directed against monasteries and churches. They coveted their treasures of gold and silver; and despising their more valuable ones of learning, they made use of books in setting fire to the monasteries. Northumbria became a waste. Learning was buried under the ruins of the monasteries. Men forgot every art of peace. To preserve their lives, hunt in the forest, and fight the Dane became their sole occupation. They even forgot their Christianity. Contact with their heathen kinsmen aroused in them heathen recollections, and they reverted to their old heathen customs and practices. English life went back three centuries.

I.—ALFRED THE GREAT.

ALFRED (849–901) checks the Dane. After struggles and adventures more frequent in the sphere of fiction than in the domain of sober history, he establishes his kingdom of Wessex on a secure footing. His next step was to repair the evils of war. He gives his people wise laws; he sees that they are administered with justice; he becomes the terror of the evil-doer and the unjust judge. But he is not satisfied to live for his day alone. He wishes to lay a foundation on which posterity may build. He finds his people, lay and clerical, steeped in ignorance; he sets about remedying the evil. "So general was the decay of learning," says he, "that there were very few on this side the Humber who could understand their rituals in English or translate a letter from Latin into English; and I believe there were not many beyond the Humber. There were so few of them that I can not remember a single one south of the Thames when I came to the throne."[1] He establishes schools and monasteries and convents. But the religious spirit has become extinct. He can not get free English subjects to become monks and inhabit the monastery he built upon the Island of Athelney, so he has youths brought from foreign parts to be trained in the habits and discipline of the monastic life. He works in the spirit of a man with large heart and broad views. He is not tied down by prejudices of race. From Saxony, from France, from Wales he gathers around him men of learning and talent, that they may educate himself and his people.

Alfred's love for English song and English story was a passion. His mother was a Goth, his stepmother a Frank. They both brought with them the traditional song and story of their peoples. Their servants and slaves used to sing them. From his childhood Alfred had been taught them. Later he learned those of his own country, and took pride in remembering the poets who

[1] Gregory's *Pastoral*, edited for the Early English Text Society, by Professor Sweet, p. 3.

sang both the sacred and heroic songs of his English speech. He delighted in hearing his people sing them. He had his children taught them. He would have every youth able to read English writing. For this purpose he studies the Latin language late in life, and works written in it that he has learned to prize he turns into English. "It seems better to me," he says, "if ye think so, for us also to translate some books which are most needful for all men to know into the language which we can all understand, and for you to do as we very easily can if we have tranquillity enough —that is, that all the youth now in England of freemen who are rich enough to be able to devote themselves to it, be set to learn as long as they are not fit for any other occupation, until that they are well able to read English writing ; and let those be afterwards taught more in the Latin language who are to continue learning and be promoted to a higher rank."[1] These were views as enlightened as they were useful. And yet note the modesty with which they are put : "if ye think so."

Alfred translates books not only that children may learn to read English writing, but that he may also inspire the clergy with a taste for letters. *The Pastoral* of Gregory the Great he considered a most suitable manual for them in their lethargic state. Accordingly, he translated it. And in his simple, truth-telling way, he informs us how he did it : "Sometimes word by word, and sometimes according to the sense, as I had learned it from Phlegmund my archbishop, and Asser my bishop, and Grimbald my mass-priest, and John my mass-priest."[2] The teachings contained in this book he encouraged by word and deed. Ignorance in church or state had no countenance from

[1] Gregory's *Pastoral*, pp. 6, 7.   [2] *Ibid.*, p. 7.

him, while he always recognized and advanced learning.

Alfred would have his subjects acquainted with other countries and other times. A popular book at that day was the *Universal History* of Paulus Orosius, a Spanish priest. He was a friend and admirer of St. Augustine, and at the latter's suggestion undertook the writing of his history. The book suited the turbulent times in which it was written; not less so those in which Alfred's life was cast. It is a record of human miseries. It recounts all the calamities that befel men from the beginning. But it showed that over all presides a Providence. This book Alfred translates. He even makes important additions to it. He describes the geographical discoveries made by the Norwegian Othhere and the Jutlander Wulstan. Nor does he forget the history of his own people. He has the *Ecclesiastical History* of the Venerable Beda put in such language that all might read and understand it.

But the work he especially made his own was the beautiful treatise of Boëthius titled the *Consolations of Philosophy*. It was a work congenial to his thinking. He, like Boëthius, had known adversity. He had found himself more than once helpless and abandoned by his friends. The despondent thoughts that occupy Boëthius in the beginning of his work also crossed his mind. With delight did he find their solution in this book. It was to him a true consolation. Deeply did the words of the grand Roman Senator sink into his heart. They became one with his own inner sentiments. And not unfrequently does his thought soar beyond that of the Roman, especially when he speaks of the goodness and providence of God. It is an interesting study to watch the process by which Alfred, with his imperfect acquaintance of the Latin, and his own limited diction, endeavored to grasp the refined thoughts of this man who embodied in himself all the Grecian and Roman culture of his day. His ideas strain in the struggle ; he changes imagery ; he digresses ; he amplifies and paraphrases. The myths of ancient Greece and Rome are, in his straightforward expression, old lying tales—*ealdum leasum spellum.* In the rendering of the other works, the royal author had assistance ; perhaps his was the least share of the labor ; but in every line of this we can trace his pen. It is with a certain diffidence he sends it forth. He asks the reader to pray for him and not to blame him if he more rightly understands the book than he could ; " for," he adds, every man must, according to the measure of his understanding, and according to his leisure, speak that which he speaketh and do that which he doeth."[1] And certainly Alfred lived up to this saying. His word and his deed were in accord with his genius, and that seemed unwearied in its exertions. He has his kingdom to conquer ; he conquers it. He has to reform its whole political machinery ; he succeeds so effectively that to him do after-times attribute all manner of improvements. He finds his people in the lowest scale of civilization and social comfort ; he has skilled mechanics brought from the Continent to initiate them into better methods of constructing furniture and buildings. From Asser we learn that he had houses built which were "majestic and good beyond all the precedents of his ancestors."[2] He patronizes every branch of trade and industry. He lives for his people. With a clear conscience may he give this testimony of himself : "This I can now truly say, that so long as I have lived I have

[1] Proem. [2] Asser, *Life*, p. 68.

striven to live worthily, and after my death to leave my memory to my descendants in good works."¹ He has his wish. His name is as revered to-day as it was one thousand years ago. He is remembered as an able soldier, a great statesman, a wise ruler, a lover of learning, an author of repute, and a lawgiver. In the laws given by Alfred and his successors let us endeavor to read the temper of the latter part of the Old English period.

II.—Spirit of Laws.

A nation's laws are part and parcel of a nation's existence. They grow with its growth, and strengthen with its strength. This is the record of English law. It is deeply rooted in the English nature. It has grown out of its customs. It is the embodiment of the English sense of justice and liberty. "It is one of the characteristic marks of English liberty," says Blackstone, "that our common law depends upon custom; which carries this internal evidence of freedom along with it, that it probably was introduced by the common consent of the people."² We have seen how these laws originated while the English were still in their Continental homesteads. We have seen them bring the same laws and customs with them to their island home. But Christianity has broadened men's views, and taught them to look upon actions in another light and from a higher plane. And it is to Christian legislation, and not to Roman jurisprudence, that England is indebted for the improvement made in her laws at this period. And that legislation, in the course of time—slowly, almost imperceptibly—tells upon the spirit of the laws.

[1] Alfred's *Boëthius*, Cardale's Ed., p. 92.
[2] *Commentaries*, Intro., § 3, p. 50.

The COUNCILS OF THE CHURCH influence the old customs. They take the people as they find them, mere children in their ways. They treat them as children to whom it is not enough to speak in general terms. They enter into details varied and delicate on all the moral duties of the individual. They legislate for man, woman, and child. These details would shock the present public taste; in modern books they are not to be found outside the pages of moral theology. They show the great difference between the old order of things and the new. But the Councils did good to church and state. They gave organic life and growth to the new religion. They enforced discipline among the clergy, in the convents, and in the monasteries. They established regulations for the laity on matters the most personal and private. They issued instructions for them. They insisted on their renouncing all pagan vices.[1] Nor were kings exempted from their wholesome admonitions and exhortations. The marriage relations, which in heathen days were almost hopelessly mixed up, they by degrees straightened out and ameliorated. The strength and efficiency of the very race was threatened by consanguineous connections. But the church stepped in, placed her ban upon marriage within the forbidden degrees of kindred, and thus saved the English from themselves.[2] The Councils gave unity in faith and discipline to the Church in all parts of the island. They drew together more closely the ties between England and Rome. The Pope exhorts the bishops; they in turn exhort the clergy; and the clergy exhort and instruct the laity.[3] Christian principles also told upon

---

[1] "Ut reliquias paganorum vitiorum quisque abjiciat." (*Conc. Calchuith*, A. D. 785.)

[2] Wilkins' *Concilia*, I., p. 29.   [3] *Ibid.*, I., p. 35.

the laws through the personal influence of bishop and king. Thus the laws of WIHTRAED were given, in 689, in the assembly of the nobles, and in presence of the archbishop and a bishop. We are further told that all ecclesiastical orders had a voice in their formation. We trace this Church influence in the articles relating to the fasting of serfs and the keeping of holidays.[1] Again, to the Councils and personal influence of individuals, we must add the work of the confessional, as a modifying agency upon the lives and ways of the people. For public offenses a long list of penances, graded according to the nature and degree of the crime, was prepared and published. The *Penitentials* of Theodore are the best known. A noteworthy feature of these penances is the practice of adding to the fines and reparations invariably a rigid fasting. Now, when we remember how sottish the Old English were in all matters concerning meat and drink, we can not but admire the wisdom of such a regulation. It was calculated to mortify the flesh, refine men's natures, and make them more spiritual. And thus it was that the Church assisted the laws of the state in the work of elevating and civilizing this people. Soon its influence told on the spirit of legislation itself. The publishing of so many codes at different times showed that a change was going on in the body politic. "The very act of legislation," says Professor Stubbs, "implies some crisis in the history of the legislator."[2]

The English laws at first entered into details of personal injuries. ETHELBIRHT (d. 616) lays down the customs of the land concerning the penalties to be paid for wrongs done one's neighbor in his person or property.

[1] Cantù *Hist. Un.*, t. vii., p. 361.
[2] *Constitutional History of England*, vol. i., p. 194.

The laws deal entirely with stealing, fighting, wounding, and killing. "If one man slays another, let him pay twenty shillings at the opening of the grave, and forty days after let him pay all the compensation-money to the family.[1] . . . If the fore finger is cut off, eight shillings atonement; if the middle finger, four shillings; . . . if the little finger, eleven shillings. . . . For each nail, a shilling."[2] So, for each member of the body injured is there a fine proportionate to its usefulness. The laws of INI take a somewhat wider scope.[3] They protect the wife and children against the injustice of the husband: "If a man steal from his wife and children that which may be necessary for them, let him pay a fine of sixty shillings."[4] ALFRED's laws still further protect individual liberty. His last will and testament was that the English be as free as their thoughts. But he knew that there was no liberty without law. Accordingly, he labored to bring justice, and with it liberty, to the door of each free-born Englishman.[5] And with no nation in Europe was there greater liberty than with England. Thus, while gilds were encouraged and recognized by English law, they were suppressed and persecuted under Charlemagne and his successors. But we must remember that England is the native soil of the gild. It grew there out of the nature of things. When the blood ties which we found to have been the first social bond became weakened, then was formed the peace-gild. Men banded together and pledged themselves to mutual protection. Under EALHHERE (860–866) there is

---

[1] *Ethelbirhtes Domås*, § 22.
[2] *Ibid.*, §§ 54, 55.
[3] Ini abdicated and went to Rome in 725.
[4] *Ines Cyninges Domås*, § 7.
[5] Blackstone, *Commentaries*, ch. iv., p. 27.

a deed of a grant of land signed by Aethelhelm and Cneatha, gildsmen.¹ Gilds became a necessity when the Danes began to grow formidable throughout the land. Alfred's laws show them to have been firmly established in his day. "If," says one article, "a man kinless of father's kin fight and slay a man, and then if he have mother's kin, let them give a third share of the *werigeld;* a third share, his gild-brethren ; for a third share let him flee. If he have no mother's kin, let his gild-brethren pay half ; for half let him flee."² With time this spirit of liberty extends itself to the slaves. ATHELSTAN (940) made them mutually responsible for crime on the same basis of order as that extended to the free class. But we can best recognize the source of this principle when we remember that at the Council of Chalcuith the bishops bound themselves to manumit all the slaves on their estates after their death. The spirit of EDGAR's laws³ is still more Christian. Calumny was treated with rigor. The guilty one was condemned to have his tongue cut out. The wisdom of Dunstan is traceable in every line of them. And as time advances the tone of promulgation becomes still more ameliorated. ETHELRED strikes a new note when he writes : "And the ordinance of our Lord and his witan is that Christian men for all too little be not condemned to death ; but in general let mild punishments be decreed for the people's need ; and let not for a little God's handiwork and His own purchase, which He dearly bought, be destroyed." This is the first censure cast upon the old laws for condemning men to death " for all too little." It is a pleading for life. It is a recognition of the

[1] Facsimiles of Anglo-Saxon MSS. in Library of Canterbury, No. X.
[2] Alfred's Laws, §§ 27, 28.
[3] Edgar died in 975.

origin and dignity of man ; and this in spite of the disorders of the day and the growing degeneracy among all classes. For we are now arrived at a period when England is deeply sunk in barbarism only little less than that from which she was drawn by Christian influence. The Dane, in his daily habits, was more civilized than his English cousin. He seems to have been, for that day, scrupulously neat in his person. The monk of Ely, among various accusations, mentions that according to the custom of his country he combed his hair daily, bathed on Saturdays, and often changed his clothes.[1] But he gave England more than the soldier's red coat. CNUT centralized the government of the country and ruled it with wisdom. His digest of laws is based upon the ancient customs. He reproduces whatever is good and equitable in the various codes gone before. He lays stress upon the principle of justice. He would have every man do as he would be done by, in confirmation of which he invokes the authority of the Lord's Prayer. "The first thing I wish is, that man support justice and diligently suppress injustice, and that he weed out and root up every unright as best he can out of this land and establish God's right, and henceforth consider each one, poor as well as rich, worthy of Folk-right, and let him be judged with a just judgment."[2] While Ethelbirht simply lays down the law, and Alfred backs it up with the Decalogue, Cnut hints at the basis of justice upon which law stands. Such is the nature of the growth and development of Old English law. It indicates in its own way the life and thought of the people from which it came. That thought we find broadening and deepening with time.

[1] *Hist. Eliensis*, apud Gale, p 547.
[2] Cnut's *Secular Laws*, § 1.

The people have become rooted to the new homestead. In consequence, a feeling akin to a sentiment of nationality sprang up. How far that feeling found expression it remains for us now to inquire.

III.—The Sentiment of Nationality.

1. This sentiment we find nowhere developed to a passion in the Old English breast as it was in that of the Kelt. His mind was less romantic and more prosaic. That which came home to his selfishness touched him most deeply.[1] When Columkill mourns over his exile in the most impassioned strains, he expresses his love for his native land, not on account of the ease and comfort that were his, but simply for its own sake: "My foot is in my little boat, but my sad heart ever bleeds. There is a gray eye which ever turns to Erinn; but never in this life shall it see Erinn, nor her sons, nor her daughters. From the high prow I look over the sea, and great tears are in my gray eyes when I turn to Erinn—to Erinn, where the songs of the birds are so sweet, and where the clerks sing like the birds; where the young are so gentle, and the old so wise; where the great men are so noble to look at, and the women so fair to wed."[2] This is the pure ideal sentiment of nationality. We seek it in vain in the Old English poem called the *Exile's Complaint.*[3] Therein the exile bewails the loss of his friend. And friendship with the Old English was a genuine sentiment. It grew out

---

[1] "The poetic lamentations of the chronicler over the dead kings may perhaps express the feeling of the churchmen and the courtiers, but have nothing to answer to them in the case of the provincial rulers."—Stubbs's *Constitutional History of England*, vol. i., p. 213.

[2] Apud Montalembert, *Monks of the West*, vol. iii., p. 148.

[3] Exeter Book, p. 440.

of the system of companionship so prevalent in Teutonic society. Again, he contrasts his present miserable lot with the happy condition of things he left after him. But this is only selfishness; it is far removed from the national sentiment that exclaims: "Evermore shall my country be all my love.[1] . . ." But it is with unfeigned grief the poet thinks of friendship's troth, now as though it had never been plighted: "Full oft we promised that naught should part us—naught else save death alone: that is again changed, and our friendship is now as though it had not been."[2]

2. But the book most characteristic of the English genius is the *Old English Chronicle*.[3] There runs through it an undercurrent of feeling dictated by a love for recounting English deeds and an admiration for English pluck. It gives a plain, unvarnished tale. Things are stated as they happened. It is mostly a book of names and dates dryly entered; occasionally there is a piece of fine description; rarely a touching expression, and in a few instances the chronicler bursts forth into a poetical strain. The *Chronicle* dates from time immemorial. It was a general custom among the Teutonic nations to keep a record of their principal deeds. This was preserved in Runic characters. "The concurrent testimony of tradition," says Kemble, "and the evidence of actual fact, assure us that throughout Europe short inscriptions were in use, commemorative of great public events or of distinguished indi-

---

[1] "Mon pays sera mes amours
Toujours."
—Chateaubriand, *Le Montagnard Émigré*. Compare Campbell's *Exile of Erin*, and Béranger's *Le Retour dans la Patrie*.

[2] Exeter Book, p. 441.

[3] Text: The three-text edition published in the Rolls Series.

viduals."[1] But the oldest MS. of the *Chronicle*, as we now possess it, dates only from 891. It was first filled up by a Northumbrian hand.[2] Alfred gave it a new impetus. Under Archbishop PHLEGMUND it expands into an historical narrative. Then, under the Archbishops of Canterbury, it varies in interest. At the time of the Norman Conquest, it was transferred to the monastery of Peterborough, where it was continued till the death of Stephen. Such is the history of the *Chronicle*. It is racy of the soil. It is the most characteristic literary product of English thought. It gave that taste for historical research in which England shines preëminent among the nations of Europe. No other country can boast of such a vast collection of authentic historical material.[3]

The *Chronicle*, as in a mirror, reflects the various moods of the people each year. Calamities are accompanied by signs and wonders: "A. D. 793. In this year dire forewarnings came over the land of the Northumbrians, and miserably terrified the people: there were excessive whirlwinds and lightnings, and fiery dragons were seen in the air. A great famine soon followed these tokens; and a little after that, in the same year, on the VI. of the Ides of January,[4] the havoc of heathen men miserably destroyed God's church at Lindesfarne, through rapine and slaughter." Each natural phenomenon has its record. The passage of a comet is recorded in the same line with the passing of a saint and the death and succession of a king: "A. D. 729. In this

[1] *Archæologia*, vol. xxviii., p. 330.

[2] *Manual of English Literature*, by Mr. T. Arnold, p. 16.

[3] See, for instance, that rich mine now being issued by the Master of the Rolls.

[4] January 8th.

year the star comet appeared; and St. Ecgberht died in Iona. And in the same year Osric died; he was king eleven winters; then Ceolwulf succeeded to the kingdom and held it eight years. . . . A. D. 733. In this year Athelbald captured Somerton; and the sun was eclipsed, and all the sun's disk was like a black shield; and Acca was driven from his bishopric." Sometimes it is eulogistic; sometimes it finds a word of censure for those to whom it is due; sometimes it moralizes in presence of death, as when recounting the demise of William the Conqueror. Monk WULFSTAN (1007-1095), who, it is thought, was then editor of this national document, lets his personality crop out: "If any wisheth to know what manner of man he was, or in what worship he was held, or of how many lands he was lord, then will we write of him as we have known him; for we looked on him and in his household dwelt awhile." And in the same place he makes these wholesome reflections which reëcho the poem of *The Grave:* "Alas! how false and how unstable is this world's wealth! He who was before a powerful king and lord of many a land, had then of all his land only a portion of seven feet; and he who was whilom decked with gold and with gems lay there covered over with mold!"[1] Centuries after, that strain will be taken up by another Englishman, and in the same spirit Sir Walter Raleigh will repeat what is here written, and which he may have read. Speaking to Death, he says: "Thou hast drawn together all the far-stretched greatness, all the pride, cruelty, and ambition of man, and covered it all over with these two narrow words, *Hic jacet!*"[2]

Thus toil these monks. They create this people's

[1] Under A. D. 1087.
[2] *History of the World.*

civilization, they cultivate and preserve its language; they teach it refinement; their culture extends to the very soil as well as to intellect and heart. They record the glories and trials—the strength and the weakness—the shame and the honor of their race. But they have no good word for themselves; they keep in the background; their names are frequent matter of conjecture; they sought only to have them inscribed in the book of life.

3. Most forcibly is the sentiment akin to the national feeling told in the poetic efforts that run through the latter part of the *Chronicle*. These vary in merit. That on the death of Edgar is a commonplace eulogy. The very form of expressing his death is that which Old English poetry naturally assumed. In the stereotyped manner it tells that he left the joys of earth and chose him other light: "A. D. 975. Here ended the joys of earth for Edgar, King of Englishmen; he chose him other light beauteous and winsome, and left this frail, this perishable life."[1] Of superior merit is the *Battle of Brunanburh*. Passages in it recall the spirit of *Beowulf* or the war-strophes of Cedmon. The poem must have been the war-lyric of that day. It begins:

> "This year King Athelstan, the lord of earls,
> Ring-giver to the warriors, Edmund too,
> His brother, won in fight with edge of swords
> Life-long renown at Brunanburh. The sons
> Of Edward clave with the forged steel the wall
> Of linden shields. The spirit of their sires
> Made them defenders of the land, its wealth,
> Its homes, in many a fight with many a foe.
> Low lay the Scottish foes, and death-doomed fell
> The shipmen; the field streamed with warrior's blood,

[1] See Ante p. 45.

When rose at morning-tide the glorious star,
The sun, God's shining candle, until sank
The noble creature to its setting. There
Lay many a Northern warrior, struck by darts
Shot from above the shield, and scattered wide
As fled the Scots, weary and sick of war.
. . . . The hard hand-play
The Mercians refused to none who came,
Warriors with Anlaf, o'er the beating waves,
And borne in the ship's bosom, came death-doomed
To battle in that land. There lay five kings
Whom on the battle-field swords put to sleep.
And they were young. . . . .
. . . . Slaughter more than this
Was in this island never yet. Sword's edge
Never laid more men low, from what books tell.
Old chronicles, since hither from the east
Angles and Saxons, over the broad sea,
Looking for land, sought Britain—proud war-smiths
Who won the country from the conquered Welsh.[1]

In modernizing the language, we lose the force and energy of the original. The alliteration, the constant repetition of the same expression in short lines for sake of emphasis—all remind one of the hammering of swords that must have gone to make this war-play. It is a chaunt that in its day must have been soul-stirring. Cunningly did the poet weave into his lyric not only the event of Athelstan's victory, but the fact of the conquest of the chief part of the island of Britain. In the same martial spirit is written the *Fight at Maldon*. Byrhtnoth, an eldorman of Essex in 991, resists the Danes, and loses his life in the contest. Hard and well he fought. Noble and true stood his companions by

[1] Translation by Henry Morley in *Early English Writers*, vol. i., p. 420.

him. Fast and heavy fell the war-beam on the shield. This lyric was first printed by Hearne in prose form at the end of his edition of the chronicle of John of Glastonbury. The MS. was burned in the fire that was so disastrous to the Cotton Library in 1731. It comes nearest to the Homeric standard of war-songs. Dialogue and action blend; the men encourage each other; challenge is answered by defiance. The whole is related with a precision of style that is rare in Old English literature. Here is a characteristically English passage: "The hour was come when the fated warriors should fall. Shouts arose; the ravens congregated, and the eagle greedy of its food; a cry was on the earth. They darted from their hands many a stout spear; the sharpened arrows flew; the bows were busy; the buckler received the weapon's point; bitter was the fight; warriors fell on either side; the youths lay slain." And then the poet enters into details of the behavior of each. Even the cowards are not forgotten. Words seem to accumulate even as the blows. But English valor could not withstand the foe.

CHAPTER VIII.

ABINGDON.

IN spite of treaty and compromise, of the payment of Danegelt and the establishment of Danalaga, in spite of an occasional victory brilliant enough to be recorded in song, the Danes succeeded in making themselves the rulers of England. Though they imposed upon the people many of their practices and customs and personal habits, and revived old superstitions, they ended by becoming better Christians than their Christian teachers. But with war and devastation also came ignorance. The English lost all love for book-lore. The good work of Alfred was nipped in the bud. His educational reforms were only poorly carried out after his death. DUNSTAN revived them with some temporary success. Under his fostering care Glastonbury became "the great public school of England for the education of the higher classes of society."[1] Among his most zealous and accomplished disciples was ETHELWOLD. He combined in himself all the learning of the day. He had studied abroad, and had made the acquaintance of the most eminent men. He writes a treatise on the quadrature of the circle, which he ad-

[1] *Lives of the Archbishops of Canterbury*, vol. i., p. 424.

dresses to Gerbert.¹ He is an eminent educator. He is an active restorer of monastic life and monastic discipline. At the request of King Edgar he translates St. Benedict's *Rule of a Monastic Life*² into English, and in return the King gives him the manor of Southbourne.³ He restored the decayed Abbey of Abingdon, and revived in it the religious life. Soon this abbey became renowned as a center of learning. Among the first to become a pupil of Ethelwold's was Alfric.

L.—THE TWO ALFRICS.

1. From a literary point of view ALFRIC is the chief figure of this period. Not that he was in any sense a great genius, or even remarkably learned. But he took an active part in the educational and religious reforms of the day. He was imbued with the spirit of Dunstan. It grieved him to see so many priests unable to read the Sacred Scriptures in the Latin. "Once I knew," he tells us, "that a certain mass-priest who was my master at that time, had the book of Genesis, and he could scarcely understand Latin."⁴ So he translates the Heptateuch, the Book of Job, and other portions of the Holy Scriptures into his mother-tongue. He gave his countrymen what might be called the first Latin-English dictionary. Accompanying Ethelwold to Winchester, when the latter was made bishop of that see, he helped considerably by his practical teachings to spread the fame of the school there established. In all his writings he is very particular about his language. He

---

¹ This treatise is to be seen in MS. in the Bodleian Library. MS. Digby, No. 83.
² MS. Cotton, Faustina, A. X.
³ *Thomæ Eliens. Hist.*, apud Wharton, *Anglia Sacra*, vol. i., p. 604.
⁴ Preface to Alfric's Translation of Genesis.

admonishes the scribes to copy his works carefully. "He does great evil," says he, "who writes false, unless he correct it ; it is as though he turns true doctrine to false error ; therefore should every one make that straight which he before bent crooked, if he would be guiltless at God's doom."[1] Might he have in these words any allusion to the controversy raised after six hundred years over his doctrinal teachings? Be this as it may, certain it is that his warning was not heeded; for his words have been misquoted and misunderstood.

About 990 Alfric prepared his *Homilies*.[2] They are not original. They are simply translations from the sermons of various authors in the Latin, with here and there a digression. They are intended to be read to the people on Sundays and festivals. Alfric translated them with the intention of giving men correct notions of their religion, and to prepare them for the last day. It was then a general impression that the year 1000 would be the end of the world. All this Alfric tells us in his own quaint manner : "It occurred to my mind, I trust through God's grace, that I would turn the book from the Latin language into the English tongue ; not from confidence of great learning, but because I have seen and heard of much error in many English books, which unlearned men, through their simplicity, have esteemed as great wisdom ; and I regretted that they knew not nor had not the evangelical doctrines among their writings, those men only excepted who knew Latin, and these books excepted which King Alfred wisely turned from Latin into English, which are to be had. For this cause I presumed,

[1] Introduction to *Homilies*.
[2] Text : Ælfric Society Publications. Alfric's *Homilies*, vol. i., 1844 ; vol. ii., 1847. Edited by B. Thorpe.

trusting in God, to undertake this task, and also because men have need of good instruction, especially at this time, *which is the ending of this world;* and there will be many calamities among mankind before the end cometh, according to what our Lord said in the gospel."[1] The ending of the world did not arrive; but Alfric lived in the latter days of Old English letters. The *Homilies* are rather doctrinal than emotional. There is a lack of directness in them. They do not always come home to the wants of the hour. Such a stirring up as is contained in the celebrated sermon of Bishop Wulfstan is what the people needed.[2] And sometimes Alfric undertakes to make plain to his English readers and listeners the controversial points discussed on the Continent. These theological distinctions he himself was initiated into, by the monks from Corbie who were sent to England at the request of Ethelwold. He especially imbibed the doctrines of Ratramnius on the holy Eucharist. Now it happened that from the days of Scotus Eregina, the dogma of the Eucharist had been under frequent discussion. And while Catholic theologians held firmly to the belief in the Real Presence, they differed materially concerning the manner of Its existence. It was these discussions that led up to the heresy of Berengarius a few years later. A large portion of the sermon of Alfric is a translation of the treatise of Ratramnius. So long as both Ratramnius and Alfric assert the doctrines of the Church, their language is clear; it becomes obscure only when they undertake to reason upon

[1] Preface to the *Homilies.*
[2] Given in Turner's *History of the Anglo-Saxons,* b. vi., ch. xiv.; also in Wright's *Biographia Literaria,* vol. i. Mr. Wright, with Wanley, identifies Lupus with Bishop Wulfstan.

the mystery. Both say: "This sacrament is a pledge and a figure: Christ's body is truth."[1] Nor in this were they saying aught contrary to Catholic teaching. But the ring of this passage is unmistakable; it speaks the faith not only of Alfric, but of the whole Church then as now: "The bread and the wine which are hallowed through the mass of the priests, appear one thing to human understandings without, and cry another thing to believing minds within. Without they appear bread and wine, both in aspect and in taste, but they are, truly, after the hallowing, Christ's body and His blood through a ghostly mystery."[2] The disputes about Alfric clearly prove the consequences to which a disregard of time and place may lead. History must consult the one and the other. Events can not be isolated.[3]

2. Sermons and homilies were the order of the day. Many there were who delighted in writing these sermons in their mother-tongue. The period was an active one for the cultivation of Old English. Men sought to compose well and speak well. The literary revival tells upon the clergy. Among the most remarkable body of sermons that have come down to us are the *Blickling Homilies*.[4] They were composed about 979. They embody much of the traditional and legendary knowledge concerning the saints and the Blessed Virgin Mary. We are treated to a sermon on the approaching end of the world, in which men are exhorted

[1] Ratramnius's words are: Hoc corpus pignus est et species: illud veritas.

[2] *Homilies*, vol. ii., p. 269.

[3] For a full account of the doctrine of the Eucharist as treated by Alfric, see Lingard's *Antiquities of the Anglo-Saxon Church*, note N.

[4] Text: Early English Text Society Publications, part i., 1874; part ii., 1876.

to prepare for it with all due diligence.¹ St. Andrew is dealt with precisely as in the poem of *Andreas*. The account is more literal. The poetical episodes and the old epic allusions are omitted. The author, however, must have had a poet's soul. A beautiful simplicity runs through his sermons. He pictures things with lifelike reality. A characteristic instance is the sermon on the Assumption of Mary.² We are transported to the scene of her death-bed. Our Lord is there. And the apostles are there. And they speak of her great virtues and high prerogatives. All the details of preparing a corpse for burial are entered into. Then some wicked Jews would intercept the body as it was borne to the grave. But they are struck blind and they fall to the ground, and miracles are wrought at her coffin. In the mean time her soul ascends to heaven : "And then the Lord received her soul and gave it to St. Michael the archangel, and he received her soul with the prostration of all his limbs. And she had nought upon her save only a human form, and she had a soul seven times brighter than snow." The author makes no attempt to convince his hearers. He speaks to them of that which he and they believe without a shadow of doubt. Altogether, the *Blickling Homilies* are made out of more homespun material than are those of Alfric. They lack the Scriptural accuracy and the learning of Alfric's; but they more closely represent the average sermon of the day. The same is true of WULFSTAN's sermons. They are upon the topics of the hour. The good bishop brings home to his people the calamities that were befalling them. As Gildas regarded the English conquest as a punishment of the sins of his countrymen, so does Wulfstan regard the Danish invasion. Men had become

¹ X., p. 106.   ² 147.

unnatural. The strong tie of kinship was weakened: "Now, very often, the kinsman protected his kindred no more than strangers, nor the father his child, nor sometimes the child his own father, nor one brother the other." Crime and vice he denounced as sitting in places high and holy.

3. Alfric had a disciple of the same name with the surname of Beta—ALFRIC BETA. He was exclusively an educator. He continued the methods he had learned from his more celebrated master. We have seen how fond the English were of putting their subjects in the shape of question and answer. In this manner did both Alfrics teach the Latin language. They first arranged, in Old English with interlinear translation, a series of conversations on the leading trades and occupations of the day. This was enlarged and improved by the second Alfric. The *Colloquies*[1] have passed down to us one of the best and liveliest pictures of their day. We are introduced to the plowman and the shepherd and the ox-herd; we converse with the fisher, and the hunter, and the fowler, about their crafts; the merchant tells us what goods he has and how he sells them; the blacksmith, the shoemaker, and the baker have a good word each for his respective trade. And the cook tells us that if we were to send him away, and do our own cooking, then would we all be slaves and none of us lord, and moreover, he adds, "without my craft ye eat not." Finally, we have a full picture of the student's life. He tells us the hour of rising and the time spent in prayer and study; he tells us what he eats and what he drinks; he tells us where he sleeps, and how sometimes he arises when he hears the matin knell, "and sometimes my teacher awakens me roughly—*stithlice*—with a rod."

[1] Text: Thorpe's *Analecta Anglo-Saxonica*.

Being asked what he drinks at meals, he answers: "Ale, if I have it, or water if I have no ale." Wine he considers a rather costly drink: "I am not so rich that I might buy me wine; and wine is not a drink for children or foolish persons, but for elders and the wise." In those days, too, was there a code of honor among students. The scholar is asked and replies as follows: "Were you beaten to-day? I was not, for I was very careful. And how about your companions? Why ask me of them? I dare not disclose our secrets—*Ic ne dear yppan thê dêglu ûre.* Each one knows if he were beaten or no—*Ânrâ gehwilc wât gif hê beswungen waes oththe nâ.*" Thus it is that this little book serves a purpose far different from that intended by Alfric Beta. It raises the curtain of time and transports us back to the inner life and thought of a past civilization.

II.—TENTH CENTURY POETRY.

1. To speak generally, this period may be set down as a period of moralizing, of translating, and of paraphrasing. Men seek to bring the science, the learning, the religious teachings of the day within the grasp of the many. Euclid is studied in English; Beda's scientific treatises are read in English; church-hymns are sung in English. BRIDFORTH (fl. 980) won renown as the most eminent English mathematician of the latter part of the tenth century.[1] The name and the writings of Alfred continued to be revered; and one admirer of his turned his prose translation of the verses of Boëthius into corresponding verse, and called it *Alfred's Meters*. And men forgot Alfred's wisdom and his practical cast of mind so far as to think that in the midst of his mani-

---

[1] Wright, *Biog. Brit. Lit.*, vol. i.

fold occupations he could have amused himself in writing such weak poems. So they said Alfred wrote them.[1] Again, for educational purposes, interlinear translations became popular. It is thus we have Latin church-hymns with an Old English glossary between lines;[2] and the Gospels were so interlineated. It is from this early practice that has passed into our English speech the custom of calling any effort to go back of what is written and get at the unexpressed meaning or intention of the writer, "reading between lines." The poetry of this period must have been abundant, though of an inferior order. In 979, the Council held under Dunstan decrees that men abstain from fabulous readings; that on holidays they forbear from heathenish songs and diabolical sports; and that no priest be a common rhymer.[3] This shows that such things were carried to excess. But what these heathenish songs or fabulous readings were is beyond our knowing at present. The only poetry of this time that has come down to us is of a devotional or moral character; and that same lacks the inspiration of genius.[4] The Old English were devoted to the Blessed Virgin Mary. As early as 680 the Council of Hatfield proclaimed Mary to be properly and truly the Mother of God, retaining indissolubly her vir-

[1] "They were probably composed by some obscure writer of the tenth century, who imagined that Alfred's version of Boëthius was imperfect so long as the meters were only given in prose." Wright, *Biog. Brit. Lit.*, p. 400.

[2] *Latin Hymns of the Anglo-Saxon Church, with Interlinear Anglo-Saxon Glossary.* From a MS. of the eleventh century, in the library of the Dean and Chapter of Durham, published by the Surtees Society.

[3] Wilkins's *Concilia*, i., p. 225.

[4] It is contained in the MS. presented by Bishop Leofric to the Exeter Cathedral; hence called the Exeter Book, or *Codex Exoniensis*.

ginity even after the birth of the Saviour.[1] The Old English poet, in contemplating the *Incarnation*, thus rhapsodizes on the Mother of God: "O thou Mary, of this midworld, the purest woman upon earth of those who have been throughout all ages; all men endowed with speech, blithe of mood, say how with right thou art Bride of the most excellent Lord of heaven. So also the highest in the heavens, also Christ's disciples, say and sing that thou, with holy virtues, art Lady of the glory-host, and of mundane natures under the heavens and of hell's inmates. For that thou, alone of all mankind, nobly didst resolve; boldly devising, that thou thy maidenhood to the Lord wouldst bring and give without sins. . . . Now we before thy Child gaze in our mind; intercede for us now with bold words, that He let us not any longer obey error in this vale of death, but that He convey us into the Father's kingdom, where sorrowless we may after dwell in glory with the God of hosts."[2] Even in its hymns of piety this childish intellect must attempt to solve riddles. Here is one in a poem on the *Nativity*. We are told that at the ascension the angels appeared in white robes. Now, our poet wishes to know why, "when the Almighty was born through a state of purity, after that He Mary, choice of maidens, illustrious damsel, for mother chose—that there, clad in white robes angels appeared not? . . . Yet in books it saith not that they in white robes appeared."[3] In the poem on the *Ascension*, we find an idea couched in the old epic phraseology: "The adversaries might not in battle prosper—in the hurling of

---

[1] Wilkins's *Concilia*, i., p. 53; Rev. T. E. Bridgett, *Our Lady's Dowry*, p. 39.
[2] *Codex Exoniensis*, p. 17.
[3] *Ibid.*, p. 29.

weapons—when the King of Glory, heaven's kingdom's chief—waged war against his ancient foes with his sole might, when from captivity he drew forth of spoils the greatest, from the foe's city numberless people."[1] The picture is that of an English chief taking with him the cattle and slaves that he has wrested from his conquered foe, imaged, be it said, with devotion and reverence.

2. The *Hymn of Praise* marks a new turn taken by the Old English mind. It shows that war and piracy have ceased to be men's all-absorbing thought. Wisdom and book-lore and science and eloquence take precedence of the sterner labors. "Then honored us He who this world created—God's Spirit-Son—and gave us grace above with angels—seats eternal—and also manifold wisdom of thought sowed and set in the minds—*sefan*—of men. To one eloquence he wisely sendeth into his intellect through his mouth's guest, noble understanding. . . . One can the harp awake; . . . one can Divine law rightly expound; . . . one can tell of the star's course; . . . one can cunningly verbal utterance write. To one success in battle He giveth, when the shaft-shower, over the shield's defense, warriors send; . . . one can boldly over the salt sea the vessel drive; . . . one can the tree—lofty steep—ascend; . . . one can work a steeled sword; . . . one knoweth the course of the fields."[2] This is the religious view of man's duties. Now it so happens that we are enabled to present our readers with the secular side of the callings of life. It includes the lawful and, like gambling, the unlawful. The poem is on the *Various Fortunes of Men*. "The Lord allots various callings to all : to one success

[1] *Codex Exoniensis*, p. 35.
[2] *Ibid.*, p. 41.

in war, stern battle-play ; to one in casting or shooting bright glory ; to one skill at tables, cunning at the colored board. Some doctors wise become—*bóceras ;* for one a wondrous skill in goldsmith's art is provided ; full oft he decorates and well adorns a powerful king's noble, and he to him gives broad land in recompense, and he joyfully receives it. One shall give pleasure to man in company at beer-delight—the bench-sitters—where there is great joy of drinkers ; . . . one is very strenuous, has a cunning play of merry deeds, a gift before men, light and pliable of limb. . . . One shall sit with the harp at his lord's feet, money receive, and ever quickly with rapid flexions send forth a loud sound. . . . One shall tame the wild bird proud—the hawk on his hand—till that the martial swallow becomes gentle."[1] Such were the avocations both religious and secular poet thought worth singing. The poems throw additional light on the tastes and occupations of those distant days.

3. But England had other forms of thought, though they were not indigenous to her people. They were popular throughout Christendom, and seem to have had a Greek, perhaps an Asiatic, origin. They are known as *Bestiaries*. But where the Latin text is concise, the English paraphrase is diffuse and labored. It was a favorite manner of teaching moral truth with the early Churchmen.[2] They were pleased to draw parables from the habits of the animal creation. Nor was it to them a matter of moment that some of the animals were

[1] *Codex Exoniensis*, p. 331-2.

[2] See Wright's edition of a Bestiary in Norman French, translated by Philippe de Thaun, " for the honor of a jewel, who is a very handsome woman ; Aliz is she named, a queen is she crowned—Queen of England."—(*Popular Treatises on Science*, p. 75.)

fabled and the habits of others feigned. The moral truth remained equally convincing. Thus we have the poem of the *Phœnix*.[1] The terrestrial paradise in which it lives is described. We are told the manner in which it rises out of its own ashes quite rejuvenated. And then the moral is drawn. We have the poem of the *Panther*.[2] His skin is variegated with all colors. He likes all living things save the serpent. So is the Lord kind to everything in life except Satan, the old serpent. Then we have the poem on the *Whale*.[3] The whale was a very popular subject for allegory in the Middle Ages. The whale's mouth was the stereotyped representative of the jaws of hell in description and in picture and in the scenic accompaniments of the miracle-plays. This poem speaks of him as being so large that he is taken for an island, and ships anchor by him. Here is a reproduction of the incident told of Sinbad the Sailor in the *Arabian Nights' Entertainment*. We are further informed that this monster beguiles little fishes into his mouth and devours them. Then follows the moral, spun out to impressive lengths, that even so does the devil beguile souls, and devour them.

4. Foreign influence is blending more and more in English letters to the immediate disadvantage of English thought. The new grooves of thinking are not congenial to the English mind. Foreign influence is ruling the monasteries; foreign influence is beginning to make itself felt in the Church; foreign influence is gathering round the court. Edward brings from Rouen Norman tastes and Norman ideas. The very dry legal deeds

---

[1] *Codex Exoniensis*.
[2] *Popular Treatises on Science*, p. 356.
[3] *Ibid.*, p. 364.

indicate a change in thought and manner of wording. Their expression is entirely alien to the Old English homely way of putting things. We have before us a deed of the grant of land made by King Edward to Eadulf, his thegn. It is such as might have been worded in the latter days of the Roman Empire. The writer of it must have been imbued with classic studies. He speaks of Olympus and the nod of the Archruler. The deed begins in the usual form: "Our Lord Jesus Christ reigneth." Then it proceeds in this strain: "While all creatures were in the beginning fashioned and created beautiful by the providence of the Archruler, who maketh in many modes and divers forms Olympus, with the stars, to be revolved at his nod.[1]" Here follow the details of the grant. We have come upon a time of revolution within the kingdom and without it. The Godwins surround Edward and set the whole island in a flame. Edward dies; Harold is defeated at Senlac; the Norman rules England, and the curfew tolls the death-knell of Old English letters and ultimately of the Old English language.

Conclusion.

We have endeavored to trace the growth and development of English literature from the first dawnings of history to the Norman Conquest. In the fragments which have been snatched from the ravages of time we have studied the spirit that dictated them and the mode of life that made them congenial. We have glanced at

---

[1] "Ac multis modis ac diversis speciebus olymphum cum sideribus rotari suo nutu perficicris." Deed of Eadweard in 1049, *Fac-Similes of Anglo-Saxon MSS.*, MSS. at Canterbury photozincographed by Lieutenant-General J. Cameron, Director of the General Ordnance Survey.

CONCLUSION.   207

the manners and customs, the laws and the songs of the English people while it still dwelt in its Continental homestead. Many of these we found common to all the Teutonic races, others were peculiar to the English.[1] We found this people to have epic poems and war-songs and an historical record so far back that it were useless to name a definite period. We saw this people transplant its whole organic constitution to the insular homestead. We saw it confront and partially subjugate another and a kindred race with other manners, other customs, and a different cast of mind and temperament, and we studied the dispositions of each in the light of the other. We traced Keltic influence on English and Continental literature long before English exclusiveness is broken through and Keltic blood tells upon Teutonic character. The English were Christianized. We pointed out the traits of similarity and of difference which existed in the old creed and the new. We watched the civilizing progress of the Christian influence. This people, profoundly religious even in its paganism, becomes enthusiastically so in the true religion. It creates a Christian epic in the Song of Cedmon. It sends abroad missionaries who convert the kin it left in the Continental home. There too the religious spirit bursts forth in poetry, the fragments of which are too few. Of the poem corresponding to Cedmon's *Paraphrase* we have only the beginning, now known as the *Weissenbrunn Hymn*. And the first part of that is but slightly differ-

---

[1] See *Statistique Judiciaire des Francs, des Anglo-Saxons et autres Peuples du Moyen-Age*, par M. Moreau de Jonnès, in the *Séances et Travaux de l'Académie des Sciences Morales et Politiques*, Comptes Rendus, 1852–3. See also the discussion that followed the reading of this instructive paper, exhaustive on every topic but the influence of Christianity upon Salic and Saxon laws.

ent from the cosmogony of the northern mythology. It expresses the idea that God created from nothingness with clearness. "Questioning sages, wisest of men, I learned that earth was not, nor heaven above, nor tree, nor was there mountain, nor any star, nor did sun shine, nor moon give light, nor was there the vast sea. Then was there nought from end to end of the universe. But there existed the one Almighty God, most merciful to man, and with Him were also many Godlike spirits."[1] This is eminently Christian.

When by means of these paraphrasings and Christian cosmogonies men got a taste for the Sacred Scriptures, these books were translated into all the Teutonic dialects—into English and Frankish, and Old Saxon and Gothic—and thus the Bible became the basis of Teutonic literature. This is a fact worthy to be remembered. It is a clew to other literary phenomena.

We have found that after England had become Christian her literature became preëminently religious. Theodore added to the store of common knowledge the traditions of the East. Aldhelm sang some of these traditions and praised virginity. Benedict Biscop improved the tastes of his countrymen. He brought books and pictures and music and singers and artists and arti-

---

[1] "Dah chifregin ih mit firahim, firiwizzo mcista,
Dat cro ni was, noh uf himil,
Noh paum noh pereg ni was,
Ni [sterro] nohheinig, noh sunna ni sccin,
Noh mano ni liubta, noh der mareo seo;
Do dar niwiht ni was, enteo ni wenteo,
Enti do was der eino Almahtico Cot
Manno miltisto, enti (dar warun auh) manahe mit inan Cootlice Geista."

The *Hymn* as copied by Grimm in 1812, in Weissenbrunn, Franconia, whence its name.

ficers from the Continent to instruct them in the mechanic and liberal arts and to build for them better houses. And Aldfred, the learned King of Northumbria, generously seconded his efforts. We see him at one time giving him nine hundred acres of land for a geographical book. We have seen Wearmouth and Jarrow shed luster, not only on England, but on the whole of Western Europe. Beda is the brightest light of his age. Alcwin reflects that light in France, and transplants the methods of Beda and Archbishop Ecgberht on the banks of the Rhine. England becomes the educator of Western Europe. Then came the Dane. He destroys in a short time the accumulated labors of centuries. In seven short years he has sacked and burned every monastery and convent in Northumbria. What was a garden of peace and saintliness becomes a desert waste. Alfred checks his course, and makes Winchester another focus of learning. Again the light wanes; then it revives under the fostering care of Dunstan and Ethelwold and Alfric; Glastonbury, and Abingdon, and Winchester become each a celebrated seat and nursery of scholars and zealous monks and clergy. But the Norman despises the Old English language; it ceases to be written, and soon runs waste into as many dialects as there are shires, till Old English literature is extinguished in the last entry of the *Chronicle*.

Such, in a few words, is the record of the rise and fall of Old English literature. We have found beneath it change, and growth, and development. With Christianity came a new civilization and a new order of ideas. Tastes were cultivated, manners refined, views broadened, and natures spiritualized. But the work is still imperfect. Many elements are lacking. In all that remains of Old English literature, we have met with no trace of mirth, or wit, or humor, or the sentiments of love and patriotism—sentiments the essence of which is total forgetfulness of self and absorption in the object of one's affections. In the stead, we have found a grave seriousness, a robust energy, love of war, a religious nature, and an unconquerable selfishness; we have found a slow-moving intelligence and a corresponding utterance. English life, political, social, and intellectual, is still in its infancy.

INDEX.

A

	PAGE
Abingdon	198
Adrian	182
Aidann	91
Alcwin	161
his genius and influence as an educator	162, 163
Aldfred, King of Northumbria	158, 209
Aldhelm (656–719)	133, 159
his style	134
his praise of virginity	134
he writes Old English poems	135
probable author of *Andreas*	136
Alfred's Meters, not written by Alfred the Great	200
Alfred the Great (849–901)	175
he checks the Danes	175
he encourages learning	176
his love for Old English song	176
his desire to see all his subjects educated	177
he translates Gregory's *Pastoral*	177
he translates Boëthius's *Consolations of Philosophy*	178
the benefactor of his people	179
his laws	183
Alfric	194
his *Homilies*	195
Alfric Bota	199
his *Colloquies*	199
Andreas	136, 198
Aneurin (510–560)	66
Arabian Nights' Entertainment	205
Arnold, Matthew, Keltic influence on English poetry	59
Arnold, T., on *Beowulf* (note)	46

	PAGE
Aryan and English, their kinship	6
Ascension, hymn of the	202
Asser	177
Athelstan	184
Athens	13
Augustin	84
books he brings to England	85
Aurelius Conanus	63
Avitus	18

B

	PAGE
Baldr, legend of	92
Battle of Brunanburh	190
Beda (672–735)	18, 153
his school	154
his knowledge	155
his writings	154, 156
his death	157
Benedict Biscop	152
Beowulf: an Old English epic	89
analysis of the poem	39–44
it is composed of two cycles	42
the dragon-cycle	42–44
theories concerning the poem	44
its present shape accounted for	46
its ideal	47
Bernard, St., on the Immaculate Conception	75
Bestiaries	204
Boëthius, *Consolations of Philosophy*	178
Boniface	159
Brecca	9
Bridforth	200
Brutus, story of, preserved by the Kymry	61
Byrhtnoth	15

INDEX.

C

	PAGE
Canon of literary criticism	8
Canterbury	131
Carausius employs Frankish mercenaries	58
Cedd	91
Cedmon: Palgrave's theory concerning (note)	97
story of his life unraveled	100
the songs he will not sing	101
his call to the religious life	103
he devotes himself to religious poetry	104
origin of the story that he was an illiterate workingman	105
he sings of the Holy Rood	107
he bewails the passing away of his friends	108
secret of his success	110
his death-bed	112
he paraphrases the sacred Scriptures	114
his Satan compared with Milton's	119
his description of the destruction of Pharaoh and his host	122
his influence at home	123
his influence abroad	125
Chaldean mythology identical in its first principle with Teutonic	50
Charm for sprained limb	94
Christian version of	95
Chrestien of Troyes	78
Cnut, his laws	185
Coifi	87
Colloquies of Alfric Beta	199
Columkill	90, 186
Continental homestead	5
Councils of the Church in England	181
Creidé, the beautiful	78
Cynewulf	140
his poem of *Elene*	141
his poem of *St. Juliana*	143
his *Last Judgment*	144

D

Danes	175
Deor, his character and poem	35-37

	PAGE
Duel, the, prevalent among the Teutonic races	18, 19
Dujon	129
Duns Scotus	75
Dunstan	193

E

Ebel on the affinity between Keltic and Teutonic languages	57
Edain, Queen, the legend of	74
Edda, the, on woman	27
Edgar: his laws	184
death of	190
Edwards on the infusion of Keltic blood among the English	58
Edward the Confessor	205, 206
Egil	25
England's relapse to paganism	83
English: on their Continental homestead	5-56
soil, climate, and character	6
Eorls and ceorls	15
Eostre	93
Ethelbirht, laws of	182
Etheldrida, Queen	157
Ethelred, his laws	184
Ethelwold	193
Exile's Complaint	186

F

Ferdiad and Cuchulaind	69
Fight at Finnesburgh	87, 88
Fight at Maldon	191
Food of the Old English	32
Frankish mercenaries in Britain under Carausius	58

G

Gaedhil and Kymry	63
Gildas	61
his fierce invectives	62
his Epistle characterized	63
Gnomic Verses	169
Gondebaud	13
Grave, The	170
Gregory the Great (550-604)	79
his administrative genius	81, 82
his writings	82, 83

www.ingramcontent.com/pod-product-compliance
Lightning Source LLC
Chambersburg PA
CBHW031827230426
43669CB00009B/1248